UNCERTAIN FLIGHT

Monica Knott

River's Bend Press

Uncertain Flight
Copyright © 2008 Monica Knott.

First Edition
ISBN 978-0-9729445-7-1

River's Bend Press
Post Office Box 606
Stillwater, Minnesota 55082 USA
www.riversbendpress.com

Edited by Wm. Schmaltz

All rights reserved. No part of this book may be reproduced or transmitted in any form or by any Means, electronic, or mechanical, including photo-copying, recording, or by any information storage and retrieval system, except for brief excerpts for review purposes, without written permission from the publisher.

The paper used in this publication meets the minimum requirements of the American National Standard for Information Sciences – Permanence of Paper for printed Library Materials, ANSI Z39.48-1992

Cover design by Joseph Gillette

Library of Congress Cataloging-in-Publication Data

Knott, Monica.
Uncertain flight / by Monica Knott. -- 1st ed.
p. cm.
ISBN-13: 978-0-9729445-7-1 (alk. paper)
ISBN-10: 0-9729445-7-5 (alk. paper)
1. Knott, Monica--Childhood and youth. 2. German Americans--Biography. 3. Immigrants--United States--Biography. 4. World War, 1939-1945--Personal narratives, German. 5. World War, 1939-1945--Refugees--Germany. 6. Refugees--Germany--Biography. 7. Hildesheim (Germany)--Biography. I. Title.
E184.G3K625 2008
940.53086'914--dc22
20070527442

This book is dedicated to my parents,
my siblings and my children.

Acknowledgements:

First, I especially want to thank Hedwig, who has answered dozens of phone calls and hundreds of questions over the years. Also, I want to thank my brother Juergen, who doubted that I would ever finish the book but he patiently answered scores of questions anyway. I would also like to thank the late Jay Smith and his daughter Amy for their encouragement and assistance, as well as Professors Dr. Richard Shreve, Dr. Jerry Moore, Dr. Duncan and professor Singer, who really believed in this project. I also would like to thank my friends, whose interest and enthusiasm sustained me throughout this long process: Rolf Haas, Mari Taussig, Don Cline, Della Ebe, Herb Ebe, Calvin Ettel, John Granville, Mary Guizze, Mosie Rikand, Richard Roberts, Renate Schmidt, Anneliese Fischer, Renate Hentsschel from Germany, Daniel Scott, Joan Vanderbett, and Will York. I thank my mother Wally Breitkopf, who died at the beginning of the project in 2003, but without whose memory I could not have completed the manuscript. I could not have written this book without the assistance of my children, John and Tanja. Lastly, I would like to thank Dr. Vincent Casaregola of Saint Louis University, who introduced me to my assistant Bob Blaskiewicz, and Jack Knott. Without Bob and Jack, this book simply would not have been complete.

Introduction: Leaving Home

Everyone, at some point in life, leaves home for the first time. It is as normal and monumental an event as starting school, getting one's first job, selecting a mate, having children, retiring, and dying. It is a mark of maturity for a young person to decide to loosen one's childhood bonds to home so her fortune is no longer tied to those of others. When one makes that decision, she has grown and has rejected innocence for the adult world of experience. Once she has crossed that threshold, she can never return.

History, however, does not always allow one to decide the time or maturity to face the world on its own terms. Powers beyond one's control can force us to grow up faster than nature would suggest. As a young girl growing up in eastern Germany in the wake of the World War II, I was swept out the door of my childhood home into a sea of the displaced and dispossessed.

My fate was virtually identical to those of countless other Germans and so many millions of Jewish people who lost their lives in the concentration camps. While history will not and cannot excuse the immense sufferings inflicted on millions of Germans during World War II, all but the most intolerant and racist reviewer of the war would be hard pressed to find any fault in the children of those who brought about one of the greatest tragedies of the 20th century. By the same token, one cannot blame a child for the unquestioning love of her parents and absolute admiration for her elders, regardless of the older generations' follies.

It is only in retrospect that the child can pass judgment on her parents, since the child is completely dependent on her family for survival. This was never truer than during the war; my mother kept me and my family alive during Germany's darkest hour and deliverved us from a persecution every bit as brutal and unforgiving as that practiced by the Nazis. For that I am eternally in her debt and unwaveringly grateful.

In a very real sense, my childhood was cut short when my family was forced to leave home. By telling my story, I hope not only to give an idea of the hardships my family suffered, but also lay claim to what was taken away from me. In this way, this story is like a homecoming.

Prologue: Uncertain Flight

They say your life flashes before your eyes when you're suddenly faced with death, but I don't believe it. It has happened to me twice, and neither time did I think of the past. The first time death confronted me, I was probably too young to realize how easily I could die. Perhaps my life did pass before my eyes, but I had only been alive a short a time. I blinked and missed it. The second time death made its presence, my life certainly had longevity and I would have known it if I had seen it all again.

The second time I faced death was a day in September that I will remember for the rest of my life. That morning, my alarm clock clicked softly two seconds before the alarm sounded. I was already awake. It read 3:30 a.m. I turned on the radio and the weatherman said there would be thunderstorms in the morning, but would clear by the afternoon.

The room was chilly. It had gotten colder in the night. Rain lashed at the windows; the wind moaned under the eves. September is usually a nice time of the year to fly, but not this day. I stayed in my warm bed a bit longer and thought about my dream. My sleep had been uneasy and filled with blurry images, like a home movie. I had seen dead bodies in stark black and white. They were wrapped in quilts and had been hastily lined up in the snow.

I rolled out of bed and shook the dream away. The German word for terror was "Schrecken," (terror) and I had experienced more than my fair share. As a child, I watched my father go off to war, witnessed soldiers hiding in my mother's garden, and was shoved into a cattle train.

Enough, I thought to myself. I have to be ready for a 6 a.m. flight to Chicago. The return flight was at 8:30 a.m. This was considered a pretty normal flight, but the passengers would most likely be uneasy if the weather did not clear.

My morning routine was automatic. I turned on all of the lights in my apartment, but could not shake the night's images from my mind. I put on the pink robe that my mother sent me for my birthday. I found myself standing at the kitchen counter with a cup of coffee. I didn't see the wall I was staring at. Instead, I saw a hungry child I once knew.

Lightening flickered across the windowpane and thunder grumbled outside. Pilots and flight attendants routinely flew in this kind of weather, ignoring physics and, some would say, common sense. Falling is the only terror that new born babies experience. The other fears like snakes, spiders, loud noises, large dogs, and fires are all learned. So why was the gaunt phantom of a little boy terrifying and the chance I could fall from the sky in the next few hours was not? Maybe I was born without a fear of falling.

I was grateful the cab driver did not speak to me; I was in not in a chatty mood. There was no traffic, no sun, and the buildings of St. Louis were still dark. The only illumination came from the orange-tinged street lamps.

In my mind, I tried to organize my day, my week. This was supposed to be my twin sister, Erica's flight, but she had asked me to change flights with her. I pressed my forehead against the cool window of the cab and felt the vibrations from the road. I arrived at the airport at 5 a.m. The rain blew in sheets across the runways and thunder rolled across the concourse. I was more afraid of thunder than lightening. As a little girl, thunder would drive me to my mother's side.

The flight was going to be delayed. Delays are routine, sometimes mechanical or electrical. This was different. I wasn't afraid of what was keeping us on the ground, just irritated. The passengers would be complaining about missing their connecting flights or important business meetings. Most of them would know that I was not responsible for the delay, but surely wouldn't care and would vent their frustrations at me.

At any rate, when I arrived at the airport, I was glad to see that my favorite pilot, Captain Herb Kearn was in charge. One look at his face told me this delay was not routine and would not be fixed soon. The weather was too nasty.

On an airplane, the captain is the boss and his decisions persist. So I chatted with some of the passengers, gave out some coffee, and the smokers smoked. Some passengers milled about, some were clearly impatient. Most of them were at least a little wary of taking off in such weather. The flight was getting to be two hours late and Captain Kearn was not happy. Finally, a voice from the cockpit announced the weather had not improved as much as he would have liked, but we were going to take off, anyway.

I was the only flight attendant on the three-crew F27 Fairchild. We were going to take forty passengers into a line of thunderstorms. I had made this trip a hundred times before. I saw no reason to be concerned. I knew we would be okay as soon as we were above the clouds. At any rate, I enjoyed flying with Captain Kearn; the fact that he was the pilot was perhaps the only reason I was glad I had taken my sister's place on the schedule. He was an excellent pilot and a very pleasant man. He ran a tight ship and did not tolerate errors on the part of his flight crew. He was an authoritarian and rigid for the passenger's safety, for which he was responsible. I always felt safe flying with him, and did not even think to question his judgment when he said we were taking off. I barely noticed when we lifted off the runway.

As soon as we were in the air, however, it seemed clear that Captain Kearn expected the flight to be more difficult than most. I could tell because he paid absolutely no attention to me and focused completely on flying. The sky seemed to get darker as we ascended toward the thunderclouds. We rocked a little bit as we entered the clouds, but that still didn't bother me.

We were about halfway to Midway airport in Chicago, Illinois and approaching our highest altitude when the plane bobbled a bit. It was just a little turbulence, but it was enough for Captain Kearn to reassure the passengers over the intercom. He said the weather would probably pass, at most, in a few minutes. Almost as if to mock him, the moment he turned off his microphone, it seemed as if an enormous hand grabbed the plane and spiked it like a football. I had just fastened my belt in the jump seat, and it was the only thing that kept me from smashing into the ceiling. The plane was rocking violently and falling. Captain Kearn, I knew, was trying to get out of the turbulence, struggling to either get above or below it. Again, his voice came on the intercom. He told me to prepare for an emergency landing. I probably would have panicked like the rest of the passengers if I didn't have a checklist to follow. I wouldn't have to sweat it out like they did.

Carry-on luggage was dropping into the aisle, a couple of emergency oxygen masks had been knocked loose above the passenger's heads, and everything on my snack cart had been tossed on the floor. Those passengers who had drinks were soaked. White pillows flew about the cabin and people were grasping desperately for their sick bags. Everyone was screaming and calling for help and praying. As the call buttons kept blinking, I was worried the pitchers of hot and cold water stowed above the jump seat were going to come crashing down on me. I felt helpless, and I for sure thought we were going down.

In the cockpit, Captain Kearn was struggling to keep control of the airplane. The two-propeller plane veered crazily, and it felt like the wings were going to snap off. Eventually, after about fifteen minutes, he managed to get the aircraft under control. We landed at Midway, bruised and humbled, but alive.

The passengers filed out silently; they apparently had forgotten about their connecting flights and business meetings. They all looked pale and sick.

From the crew lounge in Chicago, I called my sister and woke her up. I told her what had happened. I struggled to explain how it felt to have the plane suddenly drop away from you and how powerless and scared I felt. I could think of little that compared to what I had just been through, but I finally settled on, "It felt like the Russians invaded our town."

Chapter One: Mother's Parties

My earliest childhood memory is of the lavish parties my mother would throw during the spring and summer in the years before the war. Erica and I were young, maybe four years old. We were stretched out on the cold wood floor in the dark at the top of the steps, staring at the light coming from downstairs. We were supposed to be on the third floor, but we could hear voices and imagine what was happening much better from the top of the steps on the second floor. We spent a long time looking down at the soft light cast against the wall at the bottom of the stairs and at the shadows that passed across it as the guests arrived.

I was perfectly silent; I did not breathe. We would come downstairs when we were called, but until then, we were supposed to be in our room playing with our brother Juergen who was a few years older. Juergen "helped" the maids take care of us. But we were all too excited to be confined to our room when so much was happening right below us. Before long, the three of us would creep stealthily downstairs to the second floor and strain to hear what was going on. One of the maids, on her way to check on us, would silently shoo us back to our rooms.

On the nights of my mother's parties, one could expect my siblings and I to be almost anywhere in the house except where we were supposed to be. My sister and I wandered the halls of the mansion restlessly in our best dresses.

As the night wore on, the sounds of the party below steadily swelled. It began before the guests arrived, as the musicians tuned their instruments and my mother gave final instructions to the maids. The doorbell chimed and the musicians began to play, as the people walked in. All of the guests arrived by seven p.m., but the noise continued to grow as they drank, forcing the musicians to play even louder. The talk and laughter of individual men and women grew bit by bit into the noise of larger groups.

Then, at my mother's request, the band struck up the dance tunes, playing loudly enough so the music would drown out the conversation. Each dance was followed by clapping and guests' suggestions for the next dance. Eventually, we heard my father's name called out, and soon the first notes of some popular song would ring out from the grand piano. The song was welcomed by the applause of the crowd. The crowd hushed for the first song, but soon father played songs that were meant to be sung. I closed my eyes and listened to the music drifting upstairs. I imagined the dances, the elegant couples, and father at the piano. These images appeared before my eyes like a fairy tale dream.

It was not as if the children were left completely unattended whenever my mother threw a party. They were incredibly complicated affairs that exerted considerable strain on the resources of the entire household. Not only was there a small army of temporary workers, cooks, musicians, movers, and wait staff who relied on my mother for instructions, but mother took it upon herself to entertain each of her guests individually.

My mother's guests were very distinguished. Collectively, they represented all segments of the German upper class: members of European royalty, important industrialists, and stars of the German stage.

When we were finally called downstairs, Hedwig, our favorite maid, presented us to mother's guests. Guided by Hedwig's hand, I made my way through the crowd. Whenever a guest seemed to take an interest in me, Hedwig introduced me. Often my mother's best friends would shake my hand politely, pat me on the head, or even give me a hug.

There was only one guest, however, who was not subject to such protocol—-Prince von Schaumburg-Lippe. Indeed, he was one with whom the protocol never varied. The Prince was a close friend of mother's, even if he was somewhat of an older gentleman. I don't know when or how they met, but it was undoubtedly within the elite social circles in which they associated. He was very wealthy and lived at any given time, on one of a number of inherited estates. Although he shared my mother's love of travel, they never vacationed together. His visits to the house always brought new tales of the places he had been most recently. One of his favorite places was Italy, which was in his opinion, home to the best motocross competitions.

When I was introduced to the Prince, I offered my hand to him and curtsied politely. Hedwig was insistent that my sister and I greet him formally. On the night of the parties, she always gave us a brief tutorial in our room on how to properly introduce ourselves. We were baffled by this formality because we were too young to understand the estate into which he had been born.

From what I heard, the conversations of my parents' guests seemed limited to subjects relating to their wealth, recreation, business, families, and health. Later, I believe I understood why they spent so much time talking about themselves instead of subjects of wider interest and importance-—it was the presence of one local dignitary whose position obliged my parents to invite him in order to avoid unwanted scrutiny.

This man was the only guest who wore a Nazi party pin on the lapel of his dinner jacket. He was the mayor of Hummelstadt. His presence, I believe, dissuaded mother's guests from speaking freely, and they limited their comments to the commonplace and uninteresting.

In the evening after the party, my mother told my father she had started converting German Marks into South African Krugerands (gold coins) to protect the family from future troubles, as she was always thinking ahead.

Much of the conversation at mother's parties was devoted to ladies discussing the marriages they were planning for their daughters. According to tradition, the wealthier members of German society understood that one of their principle responsibilities as parents was not only to provide for their female children while they were young, but also ensure they would be well taken care of as adults. To this end, the German upper class invested a great deal of energy in securing good marriages for their children. These preparations often began at a daughter's birth and were devoted to what German parents considered the outcome of successful child-rearing.

A young girl of the upper class was sent to an exclusive private school where she would acquire the social graces and sophistication that would appeal to the parents of the suitor whom her parents had selected. Good breeding was a social imperative according to mother, and I suspect that she invited Erica and me to these parties just to introduce us to the society to whom she would eventually commend us.

As Hedwig and I threaded through the groups of finely dressed guests, a man turned from Herr Ernst, a friend of my father's, to face me. His face lit up with exaggerated surprise which made me smile. He placed his hands on his knees and leaned over so that my eyes were nearly level with the bright pin on his jacket. He looked directly into my eyes, which embarrassed me slightly. "Hello, Erica, or are you Monica?" Hedwig nodded and I said, "Monica" softly. The mayor did not really know which twin I was. "You must be old enough to be in school by now?"

I nodded.

"What grade are you in?"

"Kindergarten."

"Kindergarten!" he repeated in the same exaggerated manner with which he greeted me. "You are getting so big! Do you like your teacher?"

I nodded again.

He seemed especially pleased by the fact that I liked my teacher. "Very good!" The mayor straightened himself and adjusted his jacket. He was middle-aged and not a large man. The cut of his dinner jacket made him look more solid and broad shouldered than he actually was. He had a high forehead and wore wire-rimmed spectacles and had a neat mustache. He turned to Hedwig. "I hope I will see you at the meeting on Tuesday," he said expectantly.

Hedwig straightened noticeably as he addressed her, and she assured him she would be there.

"I'm glad," remarked the mayor thoughtfully. "I really do enjoy having my neighbors over. While it's nothing like this," he added, looking around and gesturing toward my mother's other guests, "it does allow me to get to know everyone. Besides, we have a lot to talk about. For instance," he said, turning to Herr Ernst. "Herr Ernst here was just telling me about his trip to Berlin, where he saw the Führer give a speech. I was wondering, Herr Ernst, if you would be willing to share your story at the meeting?"

"Of course," he answered. Herr Ernst was the owner of Hummelstadt's only bank.

I was awed——the Führer! Everywhere you went, you heard about "the Führer." The Führer's picture was in every classroom, every public building, and in every newspaper.

On his birthday, April 20, there were celebrations going on every place; The Nazi flag flew in public everywhere. I remember how my parents hated this day, but tried to keep their emotions to themselves, being afraid that we children might say something.

My teacher always talked about "the Führer." Whenever "the Führer" spoke on the radio, an absolute silence seized my family. We instinctively refrained from playing until he was finished. I did not know what "the Führer" did, but I knew he was the most important man in the world.

"Did you meet him?" I asked Herr Ernst.

The adults laughed. "No, dear," Herr Ernst replied kindly. "I only saw him from far away, and there were so many people there to hear him, I am sure he did not see me."

We girls knew we would not be allowed to stay downstairs for very long. We always found it suspicious we were invited downstairs only minutes before our bedtime. Nevertheless, there were ways of extending our welcome. At Father's prompting, I would be asked to sing for the guests.

I never liked singing in front of crowds, but it meant I could stay a little longer. I was especially nervous when singing in front of my mother's friends when Anneliese Kupper was present, as she often was. Anneliese Kupper had been my mother's classmate when they were young, and they had often competed for leading roles in school plays. When she was a young girl, mother had a beautiful voice, which she lost as she grew older. Anneliese Kupper, however, had never lost her voice and became a very popular opera singer in Hamburg.

In a way, I admired her, not only for her beautiful voice, but also for her elegant clothing she wore to all our parties. She was my ideal, and in my dreams, I always wanted to be her. Whenever Anneliese Kupper was in the room, I was very aware that a much better singer was listening.

Unlike me, Erica could not sing at all. She even admitted it, but she never wanted to be told about it. So when it was her turn to perform, she played the accordion. She had an extraordinary talent for the instrument and was very proud of it. Often accompanied by my father at the piano, she played familiar tunes. Those guests who had not heard Erica play before were always astonished that such small fingers could play such difficult music.

When Erica finished playing, mother told Hedwig to take us upstairs. If Erica was within earshot of this order, she would protest. "But we just got here!" Though I was a little intimidated by so many adults, I felt the same way.

Erica and I had spent almost an entire week preparing for our five-minute appearance at the party. We had bickered about which dresses to wear, and we argued about which of the maids would do our hair best for the party. Five minutes, after an entire week of fuss, preparation and excitement, seemed anticlimactic.

Erica was adept at weaseling extra time out of mother, mostly through stalling. She knew mother's desire to avoid one of her temper-tantrums in front of the guests. Erica's tactics usually bought us ten or fifteen additional minutes downstairs, until Mother put her foot down or one of the maids could lure Erica into the kitchen. There, she might be dealt with out of sight. Once we were upstairs, Erica and I changed into our nightgowns and Hedwig tucked us into bed.

We were too excited to fall asleep immediately, so we listened to the sounds of music and laughter drifting upstairs. Anneliese Kupper sang to my father's accompaniment, and the party wore on late into the night, working like a lullaby, coaxing forward my dreams.

**

The next morning, my mother's staff rose early to clean the mansion. Mother had not slept well, and after a few hours, gave up trying altogether. She put on an apron and a casual blouse and went downstairs. By the time Hedwig came down, Mother had surveyed the mess left over from the night before and had prepared a plan of attack for the maids:

"There is an unidentified stain on the Oriental rug in the sitting room, and in the ballroom there are some black scuff marks on the wall at about knee height. But you can get to those later. The rugs underneath the serving tables are horribly dirty. Honestly, you would think they had eaten with their elbows last night. You might have to call a professional, but see what you can do first." Mother paused, smiled at Hedwig, and sighed.

Out of all our maids, mother had the most confidence in Hedwig, and we loved her best. She was just a girl when she came to our house, no more than eighteen years old. Hedwig was a very tall, slim pretty girl with brown medium length thick hair, pulled back with two little combs from her forehead. Her large brown eyes were definitely her best feature, and she had a beautiful smile.

Nonetheless, by the time she was nineteen, she was in charge of the mansion's housekeeping staff and answered directly to mother. From the very beginning, she performed many of the mothering functions of the household, which is probably why we were so attached to her. She played with us, let us accompany her into town to go shopping, and did as much as possible to keep us out of trouble, since she was also the one who punished us.

At that time, progressive, hands-off parenting was not generally practiced, and it was certainly not observed in our household. No, when mother's children misbehaved, she had Hedwig administer an old-fashioned fanny-paddling. Hedwig was not comfortable spanking another woman's children, but she was less contented disobeying mother.

When the sentence was passed, Hedwig would take the protesting offender(s) upstairs to their bedroom and lock them in, as she fetched the paddle. In the few minutes, before the sentence was carried out, the offender would experience every extreme of every emotion—-despair, stoicism, anger, indignation, panic, smugness, regret, and most of all, fear—-in rapid succession. Before Hedwig even returned, the child had resolved to never, ever, EVER commit the offence again.

My mother looked around the room. "Well, it could have been worse. I saw you girls managed to get all of the plates and silverware into the kitchen before you went to bed."

Hedwig nodded. "We did, Frau Doctor."

"Good. Thank you." Mother was about to turn to leave the room, but hesitated and asked," Do you think Martha will be joining us downstairs this morning?"

"No, I don't think so. She was almost ill by the time she made it to bed."

"Have you checked on her?"

"Yes, she's sleeping it off."

Mother shook her head and frowned. Martha had been with the family longer than any of the other maids, but she did not owe her long tenure to either the diligence which she brought to her job or any extraordinary skill. Mother had hired her soon after she and father had bought the house. Martha was alone in the world and struggling to get by. She was too eccentric and capricious for most employers and had never held a job for more than a few weeks. But Martha amused mother.

Initially, she was flighty, dramatic, goofy, and stubborn. Whatever thought popped into her head, it was liable to come out of her mouth. She was not really a pretty girl. Her clothes were often for the wrong season. Besides, her shorter dresses didn't compliment her heavy legs, but I thought she was fun to be around. I liked her very much.

Martha was becoming increasingly unreliable. The night before was typical of her manner. After the guests had gone, when the rest of the staff collected the plates and dishes, Martha volunteered for glasses and ashtray duty. She gathered all of the cigarette butts from the ashtrays and put them in a paper bag so she could strip them for tobacco later. As she gathered the glasses, she quickly gulped down any remaining alcohol. By the end of the night, Martha was almost completely incapacitated. Hedwig had helped her up to her room before going to sleep herself.

Now, I imagine for most employees, such behavior would have warranted immediate dismissal. However, Martha had been with the family for so long, the break could not be made cleanly. We loved her and would have been upset if she was fired. This frustrated mother, who confided this to Hedwig. Hedwig was privileged to the secrets of everyone in the household, except those of my father. Martha's scavenging for discarded drinks offended my mother's upper-class sense of dignity, propriety and professional duty.

"What is she thinking when she does things like that, Hedwig? It shows a complete lack of discretion and manners. It's disgusting. She might as well eat scraps from the garbage! Why does she bother staying here at all when it's obvious she would rather live like a beggar?"

Hedwig did not answer and started to strip the tables of their coverings.

***

During the summers of my mother's parties, Erica and I spent many days playing outside in the garden. Mother's guests always consumed an enormous amount of alcohol, champagne, wine, cognac and schnapps, all of which came from my father's huge wine cellar. The wine cellar, which was against the side of the mansion, was off limits to the children and was always locked. Hedwig had the key.

On the day after a party, a truck would pull into the circle driveway, which only the night before had been lined with expensive Mercedes'. This truck belonged to the wine merchant in Glatz, a city about one hour from Hummelstadt. When the delivery arrived, the driver would ask for Hedwig at the front door, and she would take him around to the side of the house and remove the heavy padlock. She would then leave the driver to stock the cellar and lock up when he had finished.

On this afternoon, Erica and I were playing in the garden with our best friend Helga Keitel, who often kept us from becoming bored during the cleanup after one of mother's parties. We were playing hide-and-seek and I was the seeker. There were four rules: you could hide anywhere in the front or back garden; you could not hide in the house; the seeker had to give the other girls enough time to hide; and, once you were found, you became a seeker, too. I slowly counted to ten and Erica and Helga ran off to hide. When I reached ten, I uncovered my eyes and searched the back of the garden first.

The backyard was an enormous garden with plenty of landscaped nooks and crannies to hide in. The low stone walls and lush rose bushes which lined the walkways surrounded the large marble fountain at the center of the garden provided many convenient hiding places. If you could reach the iron gate and escape into the apple orchard at the far end of the garden before the seeker finished counting, you could find any number of secret spots. Among, behind, or in the trees, you had a very good chance of being found last and winning.

I found Helga quickly. She had hidden beneath one of the benches that surrounded the fountain, thinking I would not look that close to where I had stood while counting. We searched for Erica in the garden for about ten minutes. After we looked on the porch, in the shed, in the bushes, in the orchard, and around the fountain, we still hadn't found her. We went around to the front of the house to look, just as the delivery truck pulled away. There weren't as many good hiding spots in the front yard and after a thorough search, I told Helga that Erica probably quit playing and had gone inside. Neither of us thought anything of it. We chalked it up to Erica's peculiar nature. So we played with dolls on the porch until Helga's mother came to take her home.

It is interesting that Erica was found almost the same time she was discovered missing. After Helga left, I was in the kitchen at the table watching Hedwig mop the floor. She was almost finished when she decided to change the water. She emptied the bucket into the sink, rinsed it, and put it under the spigot to fill. She fished through the cabinet beneath the sink for detergent, but could not find a bottle. "Don't walk on the floor," she warned me, and went off to the cellar to bring up some detergent.

We used the rooms downstairs mostly as storage space. One room was where we kept jars of Hedwig's homemade preserves. Another room housed the boiler, and the walls of the biggest room were lined with my father's wine collection.

I had been sitting alone at the table for a few minutes when mother came into the kitchen quickly with a curious look of concern. "Where is your sister?" she asked.

I shrugged. "Inside, I guess. She quit in the middle of hide-and-seek and went inside."

At that moment, Erica entered the kitchen, followed by an amused Hedwig. My sister's eyes were red and tears were drying on her cheeks.

"And where were you? What happened?" Mother asked Erica.

Hedwig answered for Erica, who was in no mood to speak.

"I found her in the cellar. She must have sneaked down while the man was delivering the wine."

Mother shook her head but said nothing more about it. She told Erica and me to wash up for dinner.

Erica told me the rest of the story after dinner while we were waiting to go to bed. When she ran off to hide in the front yard, she saw the cellar door was open and thought its many rooms would make a good hiding place. She went down and finding nobody there, hid in the back room behind the boiler. She thought she heard us looking for her in the cellar, but this actually had been the deliveryman carrying down his last crate of wine. She only realized it wasn't us when she heard the wooden doors clap shut and the scraping of the padlock. She emerged from her hiding place and tried the doors, but they wouldn't budge. When she couldn't reach the narrow windows at the top of the walls, she realized she was trapped.

It also occurred to her that she might be found in the part of the house she was not supposed to visit. Caught in a cruel catch-twenty two, she alternately feared being lost and discovered. Also, the wine cellar was cold--not cold enough to be dangerous, but cool enough to be uncomfortable to a little girl in a light summer dress. She began to cry and yelled for help, but the thick stone walls hopelessly muffled her voice. When she realized she could not be heard, she feared she might be stuck down there for days.

In truth, she never had any reason to worry about being locked in there for any real length of time, since Hedwig had daily business in the cellar. When Erica suddenly found herself in a situation over which she had no control, she despaired and expected the worst. When Hedwig found her three hours later, Erica was sitting on the cold stone steps by the door, sobbing and being so afraid and tired.

Chapter Two: Hummelstadt

My sister and I were born at home on September 19, 1935, in Hummelstadt, a small town near what was then the eastern border of Germany. (Hummelstadt is on the border of Germany which separates Poland and Czechoslovakia) Erica, my mother's second child, arrived after twelve hours of labor. She was not a tiny baby, but smaller than expected. Up until that point, nobody had considered there might be a second baby, but suddenly, there I was, a cute little baby girl. I wasn't quite as big as Erica, and even though she was a relatively small baby, my father nicknamed her "Dickerle," which roughly means "a little bit on the heavy side" in German. My nickname, Moni, was as short as I was, and my father called us by these names affectionately for years.

Erica and I were born in the largest private building in Hummelstadt. Hummelstadt lay at the center of two concentric rings of wooded hills, which were neatly bisected by the town's main street. Hummelstadt's principle businesses, like the bank, bakery, and Gasthaus zur Krone for instance, lined the center road.

Hummelstadt was a wonderful place for a child in the summer. It was safe and small, and all the families knew each other. Erica and I, at a young age, were allowed to seek out our own entertainment, as long as we did not stray too far from the mansion.

We lived in an enormous nineteenth-century structure, which towered five stories atop a high hill on the edge of downtown Hummelstadt. It commanded an impressive view of the town and the surrounding countryside.

On each floor, we only had direct access to three rooms from the hallway that ran the length of the mansion's north wall. If you wanted to get something from a room on the south side of the house, you would have to pass through as many as three other rooms first.

Also, unlike most modern homes, there were no large, open entryways connecting any of the rooms so one could not see what was going on in the next room. Adjoining rooms were separated by tall, heavy oak doors. Most of the floors were either hardwood or tile, and most of them were adorned with expensive hand-woven Oriental and Persian rugs, which my mother collected.

Even though the mansion was five stories high, the household lived mostly on the first and third floors. My family worked and ate on the first floor. Father's law office occupied eight rooms near the front of the house and was almost always full of people-—clients, secretaries, clerks, and lawyers.

In the years before the war, the office employed about twenty-five people. During the week, Erica, my brother Juergen, and I were not allowed to go into that part of the house. According to my father, it was already too full.

My sister and I, however, loved to play in the main hallway in front of his office. We found the long hardwood floor was an ideal surface on which to roller skate. Neither of us was very good at skating, but we learned that if only one of us wore skates, she could keep her balance by leaning on her sister, who pulled her. As a result, it was not uncommon for my father's clients to be greeted by pint-sized, screeching roller-skaters.

We also loved to slide down the wooden banister off the main staircase at the far end of the hall. If we were found goofing off near father's office (and if we were caught before escaping out of the door into the garden), we were invariably spanked.

The kitchen was easily the largest single room in the entire mansion. It occupied nearly one half of the first floor, and it was to your immediate left as you entered the front door. The kitchen floor, unlike the other rooms, was a sheet of light green tile as long as our mansion was wide. A high, hardwood oak table, where my family usually ate doubled as the counter and dominated the center of the room. Pots, pans, serving plates, utensils, dishes and ladles all hung spotless from hooks or were stacked on shelves. A large oven stuck out from the wall as you entered.

The room was well lit via the large front windows facing west. Across from the windows, there was a stubby little hall which led to three rooms through three doors. The pantry was on the left, the washroom all tiled in green was on the right, and straight ahead was the employee entrance to my father's office.

The cleanliness and orderliness of our kitchen reminds me now of the kitchen of professional restaurants, which it essentially became in the days before my mother's parties.

In the corner, against the far wall, was the radio. It was barely more than a black box, but it was very important to my family. It played loudly all day, and kept our maids company while they worked. It bid you farewell as you passed the back door to go outside and it greeted you when you returned.

In the years before World War II, all German media was controlled by the State, and citizens were forbidden to get information from any source other than the Nazi party. It was extremely dangerous to break this law. If you were caught listening to foreign broadcasts, you were liable to be imprisoned on any number of grave charges, no matter how innocent your intentions were. For this reason, the radio was always tuned to the official Party broadcast, and mother became quite angry whenever Juergen tried to get attention by changing the station.

It was not as if my family didn't realize that everything broadcast by the Party was saturated with Nazi ideology, self-aggrandizing information and anti-Semitic propaganda. We knew some genuinely useful and valid information came across the radio. Also, my parents' wariness of Nazi ideology made them particularly sensitive interpreters of these broadcasts.

For everyone in my family, with the exception of Juergen, who spent much of his free time scouring newspapers and magazines, the radio was our principle form of entertainment.

My father, Herr Doctor Wolfgang Breitkopf, was a good man and my brother Juergen's hero. He was of average height, with soft, steady eyes and unobtrusive features. He slicked his dark hair straight back in the style of the day and carried himself like a professional. His well-pressed tailor-made suits, shined shoes, and expensive cologne marked him as a successful man.

He had studied law in Breslau. He was not as refined as my mother, as she had been raised in polite society. Her mastery of the social graces was impeccable.

My father, on the other hand, had grown up in a family of teachers and was a relative newcomer to high society. Though warm and genial by nature, he was often uncomfortable in the large groups of successful people with whom my mother regularly associated. He felt more comfortable in smaller groups, where he felt free to speak candidly and confidently. He was not, however, inclined to be especially talkative or chatty, but he listened to those who were, with polite consideration. He was a reflective man and preferred to listen to conversations before joining them. When he did, he spoke in a soft voice and kept his comments brief. It was difficult for anyone to elicit a strong, emotional response from him.

My father enjoyed working out of his country manor not only because he preferred the relative peace of the country to the noise of a city, but also because it allowed him to be on more familiar terms with his clients. He often confided in my mother that his practice probably would have been larger in Berlin or Dresden, but working in the country offered a more casual and personal setting for his clients.

Early in his career, father established a reputation as a competent lawyer. He did not specialize in any single field of law, but was capable of handling nearly any legal matter, from drafting wills to defending in criminal courts. The wide variety of services he provided to clients owed significantly to the location of his practice, since there were not many lawyers in or around Hummelstadt. As a result, whenever a lawyer was needed in the area, my father was usually called. He simply had to act very diplomatically, pretending to like Hitler in order to keep his job. He was often hired by the local government (which, of course, was run by the Nazi Party at that time) to draft documents or as a consultant. Their interference with private enterprise gave him much cause to complain, but he did so only in private.

Of course, since he had only been out of law school for six months when my parents moved into the mansion, he would never have been able to set up his office there without my mother's financial backing. My father also owed several of his first important clients to my mother's social connections, but his practice also benefited from the fact that it lay between two fashionable resort towns. It was hardly inconvenient for wealthy vacationers passing through town to visit the man who handled their legal affairs. My father enjoyed sharing his house with guests, and it was not uncommon for clients to stay for a day or two in the mansion. My father thought it made good business sense to know his clients and their families, and he often spent weekends showing them the town and introducing them to his friends there.

Inevitably, father and his guests ended up at the Gasthaus zur Krone, where he would introduce them to the restaurant's owner, Herr Piehl. Father's clients seldom left at the end of the weekend without at least a few acquaintances in Hummelstadt, and they never left without an invitation to return.

The case that brought my father national renown was a local murder trial in which he defended a woman who had killed her husband with an axe. The unfortunate husband had been too drunk to defend himself at the time he was murdered and was probably asleep when his wife attacked him. The first blow was likely fatal, so the other dozen or so hits were apparently out of anger.

The trial happened to attract national attention. My father's client pleaded not-guilty by reason of insanity, a rarely successful defense. I was present for the best part of the trial (at least for me,) my father's closing argument. It was the only time I saw my father, the lawyer, arguing in court. I sat in the first row. As far as I was concerned, he captivated everyone. I had never seen my father speak so fluidly or so confidently before such a large crowd. He was like an actor performing in character; it went on for more than an hour and was delivered with such assurance, one would think he had already given it a hundred times. In the end, the woman was acquitted, and my father's national reputation had been established.

My mother, Wally Breitkopf, was as beautiful, rich, and shrewd as the most titillating soap opera character. She was born in Waldenburg in 1905 to the Wendt family, who owned the very successful furniture store Moebelhaus Wendt. She grew up and was educated among

Germany's social elite. In school, her classmates called her "Miss Germany."

She was a tall, slim woman with beautiful, long, black hair, which she curled over her high forehead. By the time she married my father, a penniless law student with no connections, among her confidants were nobility, politicians, famous stage actresses, singers, and business tycoons.

My mother was a social creature. She loved to entertain and held magnificent balls in our mansion on an almost monthly basis from late spring to early fall. She was most at ease when surrounded by powerful people, whom she considered her equals. She brokered friendships, reconciled rivals, and tugged at the strings of power masterfully.

One of the benefits of my mother's wealth was a degree of autonomy that most German women did not enjoy. She was financially independent of my father, which suited him fine. He made few demands on anyone and was not inclined to argue. Normally, a wife was expected to remain in the home to serve her family. Frau Doctor Breitkopf, on the other hand, was nobody's servant, and she certainly did not feel obliged to remain in her home or in Hummelstadt.

In the years before Hitler, my mother was accustomed to going on extended holidays with her girlfriends to Italy, France, and Switzerland. As a young woman, she visited every corner of Europe. Nonetheless, she never allowed motherhood to interfere with her travels. Her comfortable means assured her there would always be someone to supervise her children while she was away. Also, her experience in her parents' furniture store (and my father's indifference to domestic finances) gave her control over the family checkbook. Therefore, she always had ready money to spend on vacations. She never asked for permission or consulted with father before going. A few days before she left, she simply announced she was leaving and told him where she was going and when she would be back. This was really all he needed or cared to know. Father almost never went on vacation with mother.

By far, her preferred travel companion was her lifelong friend Frau Skupien, with whom she shared a special weakness for cruises. They averaged about three trips a year. In the summer, they would take the train to Hamburg, where they would board a ship for the Scandinavian countries. In the winter, they would travel south and cruise in the Mediterranean.

My mother said Frau Skupien was actually a farm girl. I thought she was a very plain looking lady but very tall. People often made fun of her big feet and she would always wear flat-heeled shoes. When she traveled with my mother, she preferred to cover her head with a scarf which embarrassed my mother. So mother would always bring an extra hat along for Mrs. Skupien. My mother was very proud of the clothing she wore; she would take many trips to Waldenburg and Breslau in order to keep up with fashion.

At some point, Frau Skupien married a man who set up his veterinary practice in the resort town Bad Dekova, happily close to his wife's best friend, Wally Breitkopf. The Skupien marriage, according to my mother, was good, even though Dr. Skupien's work often called him out of town. They frequented my mother's parties, but often Frau Skupien arrived alone. When this happened, even though she was unquestionably faithful to her husband, she never lacked male admirers.

After one of my mother's trips with Frau Skupien to the Mediterranean, mother came back with a complete new wardrobe. This was not unexpected. She always enjoyed shopping. This time, however, a strong nautical theme ran through her purchases-—a sailor's cap and neckerchief tie, white suits with stripes at the cuffs, rows of brass buttons and white, precisely pleated skirts. She never wore these items together, but mixed them in with her other outfits.

One morning not long after the trip, before my father came downstairs to open his law office, a large bouquet of roses arrived for my mother. Hedwig brought them into the kitchen where mother and I were eating breakfast. There was no indication of who had sent them. "They are from Herr Doctor?" Hedwig asked.

Mother's face was one of simultaneous shock and delight. "Oh, dear," was all she managed.

"It's not your anniversary or birthday, is it?" Hedwig asked.

"No, no," said mother, getting up and snatching the delivery receipt from the basket and stuffing it in her pocket. Mother was suddenly quite animated and seemed to put as much distance between herself and the bouquet, and didn't touch them.

Behind the door that opened directly into my father's law office, doors were audibly being unlocked and opened. My father was coming through the office to the kitchen! Mother quickly shooed Hedwig into the pantry. "If anyone asks about these," she whispered hurriedly, "they're for you from Paul."

Paul was Hedwig's boyfriend, who was serving in the army. They missed each other terribly. Hedwig looked over her shoulder in surprise as mother led her into the pantry. "I promise I'll explain later. Just put them in water like they were yours."

At that moment, the door to the office opened and father stepped into the kitchen to pick up his customary breakfast of cold meats, bread and juice to eat at his desk before the rest of the staff arrived. "Good morning, Moni," he said. "Where's Mommy?"

"In here, dear," came my mother's response from the pantry. "I'm just helping Hedwig put some flowers in water."

"Have you seen my tie-clip?" he asked. "It wasn't in any of the usual places this morning." So, the morning passed without any further disturbances.

Only years later, long after the war, did I learn of the story behind the beautiful bouquet. During her last trip to the Mediterranean, mother and Frau Skupien had become friendly with the captain of their cruise ship. He had shown my mother special attention throughout the cruise-—he upgraded their lodging to the finest on the ship, sent a complimentary bottle of wine to their stateroom, and sought out my mother's company when he was not busy. Mother appreciated this handsome man's attention and was flattered by the respect he showed her.

On the last night before returning to port in Italy, the captain invited her and Frau Skupien to dine at his table. After the meal, he asked mother to dance and she obliged. Frau Skupien said that mother returned from the dance floor as giggly as a teenager, and thought mother had developed a little crush on the captain. At the end of the night, he escorted the women to their cabin and sneaked my mother a kiss.

Erica, Juergen and I almost never went on these vacations; Juergen once had accompanied mother on a cruise to Scandinavia, where he was greatly praised and much fussed over by men who wanted to meet his mother. The only vacations my sister and I ever went on were trips to visit family. We often went to my mother's hometown, Waldenburg, to visit my grandparents and help out in the family furniture store.

The store was a cavernous warehouse, a huge three-story building with many showrooms which were visible through the great show windows in the front. The store occupied a prominent street corner and was well-known in the city.

My grandparents and my aunt Kaete lived very comfortably on the third floor. I remember their private apartments were huge with high ceilings, large windows, and hardwood floors adorned with antique furniture and hand-made Oriental carpeting. Moebelhaus Wendt had an excellent reputation and people from all over Germany shopped there.

The huge showrooms were a wonderful place for little girls to play. It was still run by the family, so whenever one of my grandparents was ill, my mother would be summoned back to help. She had worked at the store during the six years between her graduation from college and her marriage. Her sister, our Aunt Kaete, worked there, too. Aunt Kaete was sickly and somewhat slow-witted and was unable to help out when one of her parents was sick. Her spine had been curved by scoliosis, and her disability interfered with her hopes of going to the university. She lived slowly and painfully and was lucky to always have work in the family business, which she enjoyed thoroughly. She was no great businesswoman, however, and not much of a saleswoman.

My mother, on the other hand, was an excellent saleswoman. During the six years she worked at the furniture store, she had become intimately familiar not only with the day-to-day running of the business, but also with the stock, which ranged from French and English antiques to modern German designs. She could elaborate on the differences between an eighteenth-century wardrobe manufactured in America and one built at the same time in a similar style in England, to any customer who showed an interest. She was a tactful and subtle pitchwoman who strove to send her customers away with the sense that they had learned something and had made a good purchase. My Aunt Kaete, however, never followed trends in the furniture trade, and her sales pitch was limited to how many similar pieces had recently been sold and how attractive or comfortable a piece was. (My mother once remarked that Aunt Kaete probably sat in every chair in the store, since it was difficult for her to remain standing for very long). Aunt Kaete also frequently lost sight of the fact that she was ultimately there to sell furniture and would unintentionally distract customers from the business at hand by engaging them in long conversations about unimportant subjects, which occasionally dissuaded them from making a purchase.

When Erica and I visited our grandparents, mother insisted we help out at the store, too. We came downstairs each morning with mother before the store opened and took off our shoes. In the office, we put on aprons that were far too long for us and stepped into large, shaggy shoes. Actually, they were not so much shoes as they were mops. Aunt Kaete could not push a mop very well, so my grandparents bought her slippers to shuffle in so she could clean the floor of the vast showroom during lulls in business. When Erica and I were in town, however, we took over this chore and slid up and down between the displays with as much vigor and gusto as we did on roller-skates back home.

***

Although it is no longer possible, I would have preferred to remember the town of my birth as it was in the years before the war. During the summer, Hummelstadt was a beautiful little town for Germany's mobile upper class between the luxurious resort towns of Bad Reinerz and Bad Dekova. During the vacation season, a never-ending procession of expensive autos crammed the streets of the main road, bringing with them the large part of the local shopkeepers' annual incomes.

In those days, the Gasthaus zur Krone, a classy restaurant known for its excellent food and atmosphere, seemed to be a necessary stop for affluent travelers. It occupied the largest building on the street, a white three-story building with a gabled roof made of heavy dark timber. The restaurant never seemed to close; all day and late into the night, people gathered, sitting outside beneath umbrellas at round tables. Mr. Piehl, the owner of this restaurant was in his fifties, a very proud and hospitable man with hardly any education. He was of medium height and carried most of his weight around his large middle. His round smiling face was pleasant, but he had the tired eyes of experience. His ambition made him very successful. He never married. His favorite company was his huge St. Bernard, Bosel, whom he loved very much.

***

One of our favorite summer pastimes was swimming. When I was very little, I was afraid of the water because Hedwig had warned us never to get too close to the edge because we might fall in. Ever since then, I was careful to avoid the edge. Erica, however, apparently saw the threat of drowning as a challenge, and she charged the pool whenever Hedwig's attention was elsewhere, only to lose momentum at the very end to be dragged back by our nurse.

Early in the summer of 1938, Father took Erica and me to the pool to teach us how to swim. Juergen came, too. Once we reached the deck at the side of the pool, Juergen ran and jumped far out over the pool and disappeared in a geyser of water. In a second, his head popped up and he began puttering around, looking for someone to play with.

I was nervous enough just at the thought of getting close to the pool, let alone getting in the water. Erica, I think, was also worried about getting in.

"Do you see how easy it is when you know how?" my father asked encouragingly. "Does Juergen look scared?" Well, of course he didn't. But that was not very reassuring because, after all, he was three years older. Suddenly, without warning, my father picked me up under the arms and lifted me over the pool. I shrieked and began flailing and kicking, searching for anything to hold on to. I felt like I was falling, but father was lowering me gently into the water. I recoiled at the touch of the cold water on my toes and lifted my legs into the air, but it was useless as father set me into the pool. He was still holding onto me, but I was crying, terrified.

"Moni," he said softly, "Do you see the edge here, honey? Hold on to it. Hold on with both hands." Trembling, I put one hand on the top of the wall and then lunged forward with the other hand. Then his hands slipped out from under my arms and I was stranded, sobbing and pleading for him to get me.

Erica, who had been watching this scene in wide-eyed terror, stepped back as my father turned to get her. She stepped back, whimpering and begging, almost as if my father had struck me down with a hammer and she was next. Father scooped her up and set her in the water next to me. As our fingers searched the wall frantically for a more solid grip, my father leaped over our heads and crashed into the water, throwing up such a swell, it nearly startled us into letting go of the wall.

Father swam back toward his two trembling daughters until he was within our arms' reach. "Now come here, Moni," he coaxed. He was so close I only had to lean toward him and I was over his shoulder, grabbing him around the neck. "Good girl! Can you go back to the wall?" I hesitated and felt him peeling me off of him. I instinctively lunged toward the wall and held it tightly. Then he called Erica to him. She was holding onto him even before she let go of the wall. She made it back to the wall much quicker than I had.

Father called me over again, but this time he was just slightly farther away so I had to push off the wall a little to reach him. He praised me and sent me back to the wall. Erica and I alternated turns swimming out to father, who was slowly drifting away from us. Kicking and pulling ourselves along in grotesque dogpaddle fashion, we splashed across the pool to him with our eyes closed and water splashing in our faces.

It was extremely rare for mother to go anywhere with her children, much less to the pool. She usually delegated the honor of entertaining my sister and me to either Hedwig or Martha, but she was there the day that Erica and I first jumped off of the three-meter diving board. Mother's method of instruction was much more straightforward and involved far fewer stages than father's, and she did not even have to get wet. "Erica, I will give you five Deutche Marks (DM) if you jump from the diving board." That was really all the encouragement my sister needed. She was given a challenge and knew that five Marks awaited her when she met it. She marched directly to the board, stood in line and climbed to the top of the ladder when it was her turn. Without hesitation, she walked the plank and jumped. Before she even hit the water, I was jealous of her. She had jumped first, something I had not even considered doing.

Actually, I probably would not have jumped if Erica hadn't gone first. At that moment, I was certain if I had been offered the five Marks before her, I would have jumped first.

Even though mother hadn't offered me five Marks, I ignored my reservations and hesitantly walked over to the diving board and got into line. When it was my turn, I realized perhaps I really didn't want to climb up the ladder, but since there was a long line of people behind me, I was surely expected to jump. Mother was watching me from across the pool. I climbed up and avoided embarrassment.

I did not realize how high the board was until I reached the top and looked over at mother. The pool took on a strange aspect from above, and I felt slightly disorientated. I held onto the handrail as long as it was there. Past the safety rail, the board began to wobble beneath me and for a moment I felt as if I might lose my balance. I checked once more to make sure that mother was watching. I crouched as if to jump but instead stepped forward. I didn't expect to fall for so long and my arms flew out in front of me when I hit the water and they stung a little as I surfaced and swam to the edge of the pool. It didn't hurt much because I was proud and because I knew mother had watched me because she was applauding. "Did you see me, Mama?" I asked her.

"I did. You made a big splash."

I jumped off the diving board again and again, making mother watch me every time, waving to her from the edge of the board. Erica just swam in the pool; she had really only jumped for the money. One night, she snuck out of the mansion to go to the pool. She wanted to jump from the diving board again, but she forgot the pool was closed at night.

From the top of the ladder, I could see Dr. Robach, another of my father's friends, swimming the length of the pool, back and forth. Dr. Robach was thought by most of the town to be an unconventional but well-respected man. He lived relatively far from the center of Hummelstadt, a good deal farther out than my parents' mansion. He was an older man, but Dr. Robach enjoyed the physical exertion of outdoor activities. Unless he was at the Gasthaus zur Krone or running personal errands on his bicycle, one could usually find him either hiking the trails that wandered through the woods outside of Hummelstadt, walking his golden retriever, or swimming in the public pool. Usually, if he was not doing one of those things, he was out of town. He traveled often.

Although he was a popular public figure in Hummelstadt, Dr. Robach was perpetually the object of scrutiny and conjecture among the townspeople. Nobody, not even Herr Piehl, Dr. Robach's best friend, could truthfully claim to have visited Dr. Robach's house. Similarly, little was known about his family or whether or not he had ever been married.

One summer, he had been visited by a sister for several weeks. According to Herr Piehl, she wanted to move to Hummelstadt and live with him, but Dr. Robach had been against it.

Everyone agreed that he had taught history at a German university, although nobody seemed to know which one. Dr. Robach looked the part of a retired professor. He wore tiny circular glasses with thick lenses, from behind which he scrutinized you with dark, friendly eyes. He was of slight stature and bald. He wore fine suits and enjoyed smoking the expensive cigars Herr Piehl sold at the Gasthaus. He was a master conversationalist who often invited passersby to his table to discuss world affairs. He could keep them interested in the conversation for hours, until he excused himself and went home.

***

Besides swimming, another summer event we children looked forward to was my father's annual party for his office staff and the maids. I remember those warm mornings during the summer before my fifth birthday; lazy, fluffy white clouds drifted across a blue sky, like a picture on a postcard.

Hedwig would wake us a little earlier than usual so we could get ready and have extra time in the morning for Martha to do our hair. Besides the first day of school, the morning of the office party was probably the only time of the year that Hedwig had no problem getting both of us out of bed. Both my sister and I looked forward to spending a whole day with our mother and father. An entire day with them was such a special treat, we wanted to look our best. We helped Hedwig pick out our favorite pale yellow organdy dresses, and she tied bright silk ribbons into our blond pigtails.

All morning, my sister and I buzzed excitedly around the mansion and became increasingly agitated as the guests started to arrive. Father always scheduled the party on a Friday when the office would otherwise be open. Around 11 a.m., the office staff began to arrive and mother and father received them formally in the front hall, even though they saw each other everyday.

The office party was one social event in which my father was perfectly at ease and felt comfortable enough to be a genial and magnanimous host. Even though, in all outward appearances, my father's day, it had all the typical signs of careful planning that was my mother's trademark. She made all of the arrangements-—the reservations at the restaurant, the transportation to Bad Dekova, and the entertainment. My father's confidence in mother's preparation placed him at ease.

When all the guests had arrived and the bus that mother chartered pulled into the driveway. The guests filed outside and onto the bus. One of the maids made a quick sweep of the house to make sure nobody was left behind, and as soon as the driver got the all-clear, the bus started out for Bad Dekova.

The ride was relatively short. Bad Dekova was a resort town about fifteen minutes outside of Hummelstadt. Once we pulled onto the main road connecting Bad Reinerz, Hummelstadt, and Bad Dekova, Erica and I got out of our seats and looked for father. We were anxious to spend as much time as possible with him on the day of the party. We wiggled into the seat next to him or sat on his knee. If there was not enough room for both of us to sit next to him, a pushing match was certain to begin.

While I would just be disappointed if I did not get to sit next to him, Erica would absolutely not tolerate any preferential treatment I might be enjoying at her expense. Instead, she would shove me or cry, or even tell a guest to find another seat. My father sensed an Erica tantrum coming on and mentioned that Martin, an office clerk, on whom I had a terrific crush, wanted me to sit next to him. Of course, a seat or lap opened up immediately.

The restaurant was three-story building that had been converted from a small lodge into an elegant restaurant. A member of the serving staff was keeping an eye out for us on the porch and knocked on one of the black-shuttered windows before coming out to greet us. He welcomed my parents and led the party around the side of the building to a spacious tiled patio with a charming view of Bad Dekova. Tables draped in crisp, checkered cloth had been set beneath wide umbrellas. As the guests stepped off the cobblestone path running along the side of the building and onto the patio, waiters handed them glasses of champagne. Juergen, Erica, and I were offered apple cider. The whole company milled about sipping champagne and talking. Soon the announcement came that the meal was going to be served and everybody took their seats. Waiters carried heavy trays between the tables to serve us. Juergen, Erica, and I sat with Hedwig and Martha at a table near my parents. The breezy warm air carried the aroma of a full German dinner and the clatter of silverware across the patio.

After the meal, while glasses of schnapps, wine, and beer were being refilled, my father stood and gave his yearly speech to the office. He thanked his employees for their hard work, recognizing those who had done exceptional work for the office and those who had achieved important personal milestones during the past year. Then he toasted the prospects for the coming year. After this formality, he made his way among the tables and chatted with his guests.

For the rest of the afternoon, guests wandered the grounds around the restaurant and the whole affair took on the feeling of a picnic. My siblings and I played on the hill beneath the patio under Hedwig's watchful eye, while other guests took the opportunity to walk and enjoy the beautiful grounds. Before we left, a photographer gathered all of the guests together to snap a group portrait which would be distributed to all of the guests the next week. A copy of which would hang on one of the office walls.

In the autumn, Erica and I attended the local Catholic kindergarten, so close to the mansion that we could walk there unescorted every morning.

The schoolhouse was an ugly old building, stark and yellow, with tiny windows which clearly were not designed to be looked out of. It was set in the middle of town, just off of the main plaza, but it had been walled off from the outside world so one had to pass through a tall iron gate to approach the building. The overall effect was something like that of a prison. Actually, it was a convent, and the nuns who ran the girls' school lived on the upper floors. Kindergarten was held on the first floor, and class began at 8:30 a.m. when one of the nuns opened the heavy, black front door and took role as the students filed in.

We didn't have to wear uniforms, but our teachers did——they wore traditional black and white habits every day. They ran a strict school. In later years, I was surprised to find out that most kindergarteners spent much of the school day playing. This was not so at the Schwesternhaus, as the school was referred to in town. We worked, had quizzes and homework, and were punished if we did not do it.

I was easily intimidated into respecting the nuns, a mixture of fear and admiration brought on by their strictness. Their meticulousness irritated my sister and prompted her to act out in class. At the same time, she enjoyed school and sat in the first row so she could hear everything said by our teacher, a young nun with a soft voice. This made Erica's misbehavior all the more noticeable and disruptive. While the other children worked silently in their workbooks, Erica would be restless. She would shift about anxiously at her desk for about five minutes and then found any number of reasons to get out of her chair. She got up for a tissue. She had to borrow a pencil. She had to sharpen the pencil. She needed a drink of water from the fountain in the hall. She needed to use the bathroom. When she finally came back, if she did not ask to see the nurse because she had some unproven, yet debilitating disease, like a stomach ache, she would collapse into her desk and sigh heavily.

Soon the teacher grew weary of Erica's behavior and told her not get out of her chair until lunch. Erica, sensing the nun's annoyance, could sit quietly for only a few minutes. Eventually, she would need another tissue or had to sharpen her pencil again and get out of her chair.

"Erica!" the teacher would say, thumping her hand on the assignment she was grading, "What did I just tell you?"

Erica's reply was simple and mumbled: "I forgot."

I would have probably accepted my sister's explanation--she did have a very short attention span and always seemed to be doing several things at once, but it never went over well with the nuns. The teachers at the Schwesternhaus had only two punishments for offences committed at school. If you were caught out of your desk when you had been told to remain there until lunch, you were made to stand with your face to the wall in a corner at the back of the classroom. If you were heard swearing or got into a fight, you were sent down the hall to the principal's office, where the ugly nun with thick glasses who ran the place monitored you constantly. Erica spent a lot of time in the corner, but she really didn't mind——at least she was out of her desk.

Occasionally, however, Erica would cross the line and be sent to the office. I remember one occasion when Erica decided she wanted to sit in a new desk. Seats were not assigned, but students tended to sit in the same seats every day. It was understood that the desk was yours for the year. One morning, we had just come inside and were waiting for the teacher to arrive and start class. Erica noticed an empty desk more desirable than her usual one. As she gathered her things, the girl who normally sat there came in. Both of them arrived at the desk at the same time.

"I want to sit here," said Erica.

The other girl, our best friend Helga Keitel, friendship notwithstanding, wanted to keep her desk and told Erica so. Erica, however, sat down as if she had been offered the chair and paid no mind to her friend, who stood beside the desk speechless. Helga was still standing there when the teacher entered. The nun noticed Erica was in a different chair and that its usual occupant was standing beside it. The teacher asked what was going on.

"Erica took my chair," Helga explained.

"Go back to your seat, Erica," the nun ordered. "I'll have none of this."

Erica scowled, stood up, and hissed at Helga, "I hate you," said just loud enough for the nun to hear.

"We'll certainly have none of that, Erica," the nun announced sternly. "Go to the office and stay there until I come and get you." That was how Erica got sent to the principal's office before school even started.

The school day was broken up by lunch at noon. The nuns provided the meals and we ate the bland food at the long tables in the cafeteria on the first floor. The menu never changed much. Usually we ate warm pea soup under the watchful eye of the nun on lunch duty who led the thanksgiving prayer and saw to it that we ate everything on our plates. It was always the same woman. She never taught a class, but it seemed she considered eating to be an assignment as important as homework, and if you didn't clean your plate, she would teach you to, by God.

Erica often got in trouble during lunch because she was a picky eater with a strong aversion to peas in any form. Instead, she would eat her dessert first, usually from the bowls of fruit which waited for us on the tables when we arrived. Then she would drink her milk before reluctantly choking down the main course. Occasionally, we were given Himmbeerwasser instead of milk. This was a raspberry juice the nuns pressed at the convent. Erica, however, did not like the drink, and one day, when it was served to wash down the pea soup, Erica refused to eat any of it. When the lunch monitor came around at the of the meal to excuse each table individually, she saw Erica sitting in front of a cold plate of pea soup and a full glass of Himmbeerwasser. She dismissed the entire table except for Erica and made her clean up after the other students before allowing her to return to class.

School ended at 3:00. We were always restless during the last five minutes of the day, especially since the other classes always seemed to get out before us. When our clock finally reached three, we poured out into the courtyard where parents collected their children. We always walked home alone, at least until the later days of the war, when Hedwig was sent to fetch us.

***

Very few Jewish people lived in Hildesheim. Most of the people were Catholic. Not far from the downtown shopping area, there lived a Jewish middle-aged couple my parents knew and liked very much. I do remember the wife's name was Ursula. Mother had invited her often together with other ladies to our mansion for coffee and cake, playing cards in the afternoon. They had no children. The husband was a successful businessman, and his job took him to different cities like Waldenburg and Breslau. Ursula was a very elegant lady and was well liked by other ladies mother invited. She was not very tall, but built very thin and was small boned.

One day we found out this family had suddenly disappeared during the night. Nobody really knew what had happened. People talked and said they had moved to another city. Of course, much later when the war was over, everyone knew what happened to so many other Jewish people who suddenly disappeared during the night. Mother was furious.

Wealthy and very educated Jews left their country years before the war started in 1939. Many had immigrated to America and had become very successful.

My family also knew of a Jewish gentleman who owned a castle close to Hummelstadt. After he leased it, he went to Africa. That was in 1936. Then in 1939, Hitler restricted the immigration of any Jews.

***

Wintertime in Hummelstadt was not always necessarily fun for little children. Christmas, which we thought was a time devoted especially to the happiness of children, was the only exception. No matter how bitter the winter, Advent was a time of wonderful anticipation. For the first few days after Christmas, we played contentedly with our own toys and pined over the gifts our siblings had received. With the arrival of Christmas and the feast of toys, so anticipated, it always passed quickly into our memories, as did the pure pleasure of playing with recently unwrapped presents.

A German Christmas is in many ways similar to an American one, especially inside the home. Parents used many of the same types of decorations typically found in American homes, such as wreathes, holly and garland. While most Germans also decorated Christmas trees, Germans' trees were usually illuminated with burning candles instead of colored lights. German children are also visited in the night by a benevolent, gift-bearing spirit. In Germany, he is the "Christkind," or Christ child, instead of Santa Claus. The presents he left were always opened after dinner on Christmas Eve.

Outside of the home, however, one is able to distinguish more clearly a German Christmas from an American one. The most important difference is the Chriskindlmark, or Christmas market, which is erected every December in the main square of every German town.

In Hummelstadt, the center plaza was filled with red wooden booths, from which vendors sold a seemingly endless variety of carved nutcrackers, ornaments and other Christmas decorations.

The arrival of the Chriskindlmark also heralded the arrival of the traditional fare of the season, much of which is only available at the market. The most popular Christmas treat was glühwein (literally, "glow-wine"). This was a hot, sweet, spiced red wine served in paper cups in the Chriskindlmark and in heavy mugs in the taverns. It was my mother's favorite, but it was much too strong for young children. We were happy enough with the hot chocolate, gingerbread and wrapped candies of the season to ever miss it.

Going to the Christmas market with our mother was a special treat for me and my siblings. We rarely got a chance to go anywhere with her. One year, I remember the snow fell throughout our outing to the market with mother, and when we returned to the mansion, we could see the yard, the garden, the apple orchard, the town, and the hills beyond buried under a clean blanket of snow. It transformed the familiar landscape into a fresh, new world. When I look back on that afternoon, I believe I was as happy then as I could be.

Although Hummelstadt took on aspects of timeless beauty during the winter, once Christmas passed, we children usually enjoyed the picturesque scene from behind the mansion's windows. Silesian winters are dreadfully cold, and we spent the majority of the season indoors yearning for a break in the frigid weather.

The boredom was probably worse for Juergen than for me or my sister for the simple reason that he did not have a perpetual playmate his own age. At least Erica and I always had company if we wanted it. This is not to say that Juergen merely moped about the house pausing at windows and sighing. Juergen had an active imagination and spent most of the winter reading. He was also very involved in the Hitlerjugend, a Nazi youth club. It encouraged competitiveness and physical fitness, and introduced German boys to the drills, doctrine, and discipline they would eventually need to serve the fatherland. About eighty percent of German boys and girls between ten and eighteen years old belonged to the Hitlerjugend. Juergen and his friends took the Hitlerjugend very seriously.

Their meetings took place in a building on top of a hill not too far from our mansion. I can still picture this building looking out the window from the top floors. This building used to be called the "Jugend Herberge" (youth hostel). Together, they read maps and formed ranks in the backyard to practice their close-order drills and took day trips. Our parents, however, had grave reservations about his participation in the Hitlerjugend and hated to see it also interfere with his schoolwork. They didn't like Juergen joining this organization at all. It really bothered my parents that Juergen was involved. But he had to join just like any other boy at the age of ten.

One of the Nazis we knew who lived in Hummelstadt, was the group leader of the Hitler Youth. Juergen described him as a very unpleasant, domineering, bossy person. Besides being a big Nazi, there wasn't anything nice about this man. Juergen enjoyed different entertainment with other boys his age.

The Hitler Youth organization was formed in 1934. There was also the National Labor Service act, which required young people to give six months service on farms or in industries. First, it was volunteer. Later, it was mandatory. The boys in the Hitler Youth had to wear a uniform and before everyone arrived at the meeting at the "Jugend Herberge," they had to raise their right hand and say, "Heil Hitler" before they were seated.

As we twins were too young to join any organization, we often had small conversations that I didn't really understand at the time. It was called "Kindergruppe" (a group for very young children) but no uniform was required.

One morning in 1939 was the start of a beautiful day. The sun had already come up, and through the curtains that covered the huge windows in the kitchen, the room was lightened by warm rays of sunlight.

Suddenly, from the window, Hedwig noticed a black Mercedes driving up the street approaching our driveway. Right away we knew something must be wrong. Hedwig ordered us children to leave the kitchen and go up to the next floor. A short time after the doorbell rang, a tall, mean-looking Nazi stood in front of our trembling Hedwig, staring at her as if she had done something wrong. In a stuttering, scared voice, Hedwig asked, "Sir, may I help you"? He answered shortly in a harsh, unpleasant, impolite voice. "I would need to see Herr Breitkopf immediately, while he pushed himself inside the door toward the kitchen, where my father was already sitting at the table. My father got up from his seat right away, wondering what could possibly be wrong. A little intimidated, father kindly asked this tall Nazi, if he would mind proceeding to his office in the back of the mansion. The office was still closed, as it was a few minutes before 8:00 a.m. By now, the Nazi was standing very close to my father. Father's heart beat almost became audible, and he could almost feel the revolver the Nazi had in his pocket. The Nazi looked straight into his face and murmured in a loud voice that father would have to come with him right away, and he would explain more later.

In the mean time, mother came down to the kitchen, and in no time Hedwig quietly explained everything to her. Mother expected the worst now, believing if father would have stepped in that Mercedes with this Nazi, it might have been the end for him, and we would have never seen him again. By then, father still very cautious, asked the Nazi in a very soft, quiet voice if he would like a cigar. Father opened the drawer of his desk and handed him a cigar. To his surprise he accepted it, and put it in his pocket. But shortly after that, the Nazi proceeded back to business, and he again told my father he would need to leave with him, as somebody had reported him. Immediately, my father answered this had been a big mistake. Father kept repeating himself, "Sir, how could you ever think I would say something like that," as he pretended liking Hitler, which, of course, wasn't very easy to do. He hated Hitler and the Nazis. Finally, the officer must have gotten tired and bored listening to father's phrases. He turned away from my father and left the office without saying another word.

By now, some clients had showed up that morning in the waiting room. I couldn't imagine how those people thought and felt with their bulging eyes, seeing the door open and a big Nazi officer in uniform, coming out of my father's office instead of my father.

My father remembered later when he remarked about this at a meeting, with many people, saying "Der alte Nazi" (the old Nazi), referring to the Nazi who took a cigar and came to the front door. Of course, this day was one of the most stressful and scary days my father ever experienced. It was one he would never forget.

Hedwig and the other maids were as busy as ever, too busy to play with us. Besides, during winter when the entire family preferred to spend their time indoors, there was more daily tidying to do. Winter was always cause for new chores for the house staff. I remember seeing Hedwig outside on the front walkway or driveway early in the morning hacking at the ice beneath the snow with the sharp point of a garden shovel.

Erica and my favorite winter game (besides dolls) was "Shopping Spree," in which we would proceed from room to room as if we were in my grandfather's furniture store buying and selling my parents' furniture, clothing and jewelry. Each of us wanted to be the shopper, but for the most part, we took turns playing the salesgirl describing the merchandise and praising our customer's selections. Money was no object, and hardly an important concept to us little girls. Items were priced principally by their size, so while the Vermeer cost twenty DM (Deutsche Mark), the throw rug in the bathroom might cost well over fifty DM, depending on whether or not it was on sale.

Chapter Three:
War Comes to Hummelstadt

Erica was throwing a spectacular temper tantrum in the kitchen.

We had been playing with our brightly colored building blocks when I somehow angered her. Her dissatisfaction quickly whipped itself into a clamorous fury. Shrieking at the top of her lungs, she grabbed a large wooden spoon from the counter, squatted, and beat the tiles of the floor furiously, determined that the entire family, who was listening to the radio, share her indignation. When the family failed to pay attention, she charged across the room and struck my arm with the spoon.

The slap surprised me, and my eyes welled with tears of shame. I was about to start howling, too, when Juergen stepped in and snatched the spoon away from Erica. "Be quiet!" he ordered. "The Führer has invaded Poland!"

Hitler had ordered German war planes to fly across the Polish frontier and attack Warsaw, the capital of Poland in September 1939. Soon after the Soviet Union invaded Poland, which the British and French wanted to defend. The suffering of the Polish soldiers and civilians was devastating and indescribable. This struggle eventually became World War II.

Juergen's strange look scared us, and I bit my lip to staunch the yowl rising in my throat. We did not know what our response to such news should be. We didn't even know what "invaded" meant. But whatever happened, Juergen thought it was very serious.

Father pulled a stool over from the table and sat as close to the radio as he could. His lips were tight and his face was grim. He looked so frightened. Mother stood next to him with her back to the radio and her eyes closed from fear. Martha was looking nervously at her employers. They did not take much notice of us when we joined them. With the exception of the radio announcer's voice, which was crackling excitedly, the house was silent. Juergen sat down beside father and whispered to us, "It's the Blitzkrieg." I'm sure both Erica and I had I-can't-believe-it; I-didn't-think-it-would-ever-happen looks of surprise on our faces, as if we understood the unfamiliar, strangely exciting word.

At the sound of Juergen's voice, mother seemed to remember her daughters were present. "Martha, please find Hedwig," she said, looking to the door. "Have her take the girls out for a walk."

Erica's eyes lit up." I want to go to the pool," she declared.

"The pool's closed today, but perhaps Hedwig will take you to lunch."

Hedwig took us for a stroll through downtown Hummelstadt. We tugged her from store window to store window, where fashionably dressed mannequins posed alluringly with dead, white eyes. I wanted to look in the bookstore window; Erica wanted to look at clothes. Hedwig bought a paper at the newsstand.

As we neared the Gasthaus zur Krone, we saw the owner, Herr Piehl, sitting at one of the summer tables in front of the restaurant, as usual. Herr Piehl saw us at a distance and waved to us. "Hello, Hedwig!" he called out while we were still a good distance away. "How are my lovely girls today?" Hedwig returned Herr Piehl's grin, and tightening her grip on our hands, stepped up the pace.

Herr Piehl hugged Hedwig, and crouching, shook our hands in a playfully solemn way."My!" he marveled, twisting the corners of his mouth into the slightest smile, "How you are growing! Oh, before long you will be in kindergarten."

"But we already are in kindergarten," my sister informed him.

Herr Piehl pretended to look shocked. "No! It can't be!" He turned to me, "Is this true? Have you already been to kindergarten?" I nodded my head. He raised his eyebrows exaggeratedly and shook his head in disbelief. "My word, they are practically grownups, Hedwig."

"They seem to think so."

Herr Piehl turned back to us. "Have you enjoyed your summer?"

"Yes," we replied together. "Especially riding Bosel," I added.

Erica, who was entertaining the same idea, finished my thought, "May we ride Bosel, Herr Piehl?"

"Of course," he said to the girls. He then turned to Hedwig, "You will join me for a drink, won't you?" Hedwig nodded and Herr Piehl poked his head into the door of the restaurant and called, "Bosel! The princesses demand your presence!" He excused himself for a moment and went inside to pour Hedwig's drink. He returned with another snifter and was leading an enormous St. Bernard.

Bosel stood as tall as Erica and I and drooped all over-—his eyes, his jowls, his ears, and belly drooped. Erica hugged the St. Bernard around the neck and Bosel licked her face. His tail thumped against the leg of the table as we smothered him with hugs and rubbed him behind the ears.

Bosel was our best friend. He was sweet and calm and affectionate and extremely patient with children. Herr Piehl often let us ride him. Bosel did not seem to mind. We were, after all, very small, and Bosel seemed as big as a Shetland pony to us. Whenever we ate at the restaurant, we would feed him morsels of food while he rested at our feet.

Herr Piehl ducked under the umbrella and placed the drinks on the green and white checkered tablecloth. Then he picked me up and placed me on Bosel's back. Anne, a young blonde waitress, came out and walked beside me while I rode Bosel down the sidewalk.

"What do you think about the news?" Herr Piehl asked Hedwig.

Hedwig shook her head. "We're at war. It's very upsetting. Do you know if anyone else has declared war on us?"

"Not the last I heard, but they will--France and England for sure."

They didn't say anything else about the Blitzkrieg, but sipped their drinks and watched us play with Bosel.

***

At first, the war seemed to have very little effect on our lives in Hummelstadt, even after England and France joined against us. We were delighted and relieved by France's quick capitulation and by pushing the British off of the continent.

At school, our teachers talked about the war every day and explained the news to us, and the news seemed generally good.

Not long after the Germans got used to the idea of occupying France, things began to happen to my family. It began with a cable that arrived at my father's office in the summer of 1940. It threw my father into a rage, one of the very few we ever witnessed, and it frightened us. Father burst into the kitchen where Mother was talking to Hedwig and a string of profanity flew from his mouth. He had been drafted into the service! He thought it clearly ridiculous that the government would induct a man his age and in his shape—he had never been athletic, and he hadn't done much more than swim occasionally in the last several years.

Mother was upset and worried, but she nonetheless reassured father that there was no way they'd put a man his age in a fighting unit. Father's draft notice put the household in a state of anxiety, and he spent the next several days on the phone and worked late in his office.

A few weeks later, a man whom we children had never met arrived at the mansion. From the amount of luggage he brought with him, it looked as if he was going to stay for a long time. After Otto, our groundskeeper, had brought in the man's bags and the maids showed him his room, the family sat down to dinner with the newcomer. The man was slightly older than my father and gasped when he spoke. He wore a smart business suit and caught up with mother over dinner. They seemed to have known each other for a long time. His name was Hans Thienelt. Mr. Thienelt appeared to be a very elegant, educated gentleman. He was extremely tall and had beautiful teeth. I admired his naturally curly dark brown hair.

After dinner, father and his guest retired to the law office. I did not see them until the following day. In the afternoon, father took the newcomer to the Gasthaus zur Krone to meet Herr Piehl. Erica and I tagged along to visit Bosel.

Herr Piehl was outside of the restaurant as we approached. "Wolfgang, it's very good to see you," he said. "How are you and your lovely girls this afternoon?" They shook hands while my sister and I casually searched for the St. Bernard.

"We are doing very well," my father said sincerely. "My wife sends her regards."

"Herr Piehl, I would like you to meet my new business partner Hans Thienelt." The stranger was dressed in a somber suit and vest and a somber tie. The owner of the restaurant offered his hand to Thienelt, who took it. Thienelt's eyes were full of good humor. "I'm pleased to meet you, Herr Piehl."

After the introduction, Piehl ushered us into the empty restaurant and seated us at a table near the bar. He excused himself for a moment and disappeared into the kitchen. In a few minutes, he returned with a bottle of wine in one hand and a platter of crackers and caviar in the other. He placed the wine and the platter on the table, reached behind the bar and pulled out three wine glasses. He placed one before Breitkopf and Thienelt, uncorked the bottle, and poured. "I hope you enjoy this," Piehl said as he topped off his own glass. "It is a gift from my nephew who is stationed in France. He sent me a case of it and I have been waiting for an excuse to open it. He says it is the finest wine in all of France."

A waitress came out with a loaf of French bread and a bread knife. "Anne," Piehl asked her, "would you help the Frauleins Breitkopf find Bosel? I believe he was asking if they were coming to play with him today." Anne escorted us into the kitchen to hunt for the enormous dog.

Thienelt raised his glass and gave the toast: "To the German soldiers who provided us with this wine, and to victory." Thienelt and my father sipped from their glasses; Piehl took a generous swallow.

Piehl sawed off pieces of bread and passed them to his guests. "Red wine, caviar, and crusty bread—-the best France can offer."

Thienelt looked at Piehl quizzically. "With your pardon, Herr Piehl, I wouldn't say that the French exactly 'offered' it to us. We paid for this with eighteen thousand German lives. But it is very fine, indeed. Thank you for your hospitality."

My father thoughtfully examined the crimson liquid in his glass. "What about the two hundred thousand French who died in the campaign? Surely, they paid for this wine?"

The men were silent for a moment. Father changed the subject. "Herr Piehl, I wanted you to know that I have received my draft notice and I am leaving tomorrow."

"I'm sorry to hear that. Do you know where you will be going?"

"Into the Army, but where I'll end up, I don't think I'll know that until I have finished training. Herr Thienelt will take charge of the law practice in my absence. I would be very grateful if you would extend the friendship you have shown my family to Herr Thienelt while I'm gone."

Piehl smiled. "Of course." he turned to Thienelt and said with an ironic grin, "Congratulations, Herr Thienelt. It would be very difficult to find a more beautiful and provocative clientele." Thienelt and Piehl laughed, but Father fidgeted. Piehl changed the subject. "We hope you won't be away for too long. Perhaps by the time you return, we will be eating Russian Beluga."

"What do you mean by that, Piehl?" my father asked.

"I suspect Hitler will invade Russia sometime within the next year."

Thienelt set his glass on the table. "What makes you think that?"

"Dr. Robach stopped by last night and pointed out there is nowhere left for the Reich (empire) to expand. Hitler has the Low Countries. He has all the northern seaports he needs. He hasn't been able to break Britain's back and won't be able to without rebuilding the Luftwaffe. The only military rival within striking distance of the Reich is Russia."

Father looked across the table sternly. "What about the non-aggression treaty?"

Piehl chuckled and shook his head. "My dear friend," he said in a low voice, "haven't you learned by now the surest way to get into a war with Hitler is to sign a treaty with him?"

My father and Herr Thienelt were silent. Anne and Erica and I walked by the front window with Bosel. We were very happy.

***

My father spent the morning of his departure in his law office offering last-minute advice to Herr Thienelt and taking leave of the office staff. Erica and I sat on the cold, smooth floor in the hallway outside my father's office door to meet him when he came out. Hedwig had dressed me and my sister in our best (matching) dresses. Juergen had dressed himself in his Hitlerjugend uniform, and he paced the length of the hall excitedly.

Erica and I were not as enthusiastic as Juergen about Father's assignment. Father really didn't want to leave us, as he told us many times, but it wasn't his choice. It was his duty. I was near tears all morning. Erica was annoyed; she attempted to entertain herself while her siblings waited in the hall, but Hedwig would not let her go outside. Quickly bored with having nobody to play with, she returned to the hallway without a word, sat down, and sighed in exasperation.

Father came out of the office carrying a small suitcase, which contained a small number of personal effects. He said the Army would give him everything else he needed. He stooped to pick up Erica who had suddenly started to cry, and hugged her. Mother and Hedwig came out when they heard his office door open and stood by while he said goodbye to us. He hardly spoke at all. He merely told us to be good, told Juergen to take care of his sisters, gave Mother a kiss, and promised to call or write when he arrived at the induction center. He put on his hat and walked out the door. The mansion seemed much larger and emptier.

For the next several months, we occasionally received letters from father. In the letters he sent from basic training, it sounded as if he was doing many exciting things. Juergen was captivated by father's description of bayonet drills, marches, barracks, rifle practice and army food. Juergen couldn't help but talk about the great time that father must be having. At the end of his training, Father was transferred to a replacement depot in Germany, where he worked for a supply officer making sure the supplies ordered were received. Juergen was no less interested, but father mentioned his job was probably temporary and that he expected to be reassigned. Eventually, he received a permanent assignment in Wilhelmshaven as a supply officer, responsible for keeping U-boats supplied when they returned to port.

***

Saturday, June 22, 1941 was the kind of morning children like best. It was a warm, sunny day. Lazy, fluffy clouds drifted slowly across a blue sky. Suddenly, the speakers above the Provost's office popped and screeched, and the Provost's voice shattered the morning's peace:

"Men and women of Hummelstadt, your Führer, Adolf Hitler, has asked me personally to announce that troops from the Soviet Union have dared to violate our border. In blatant disregard for the non-aggression pact, Russian invasion forces have attacked the Eastern Frontier at several points and have bombed the cities of Modlin, Lublin and Danzig from the air. Germany has honored her non-aggression pact with the Soviet Union. The Soviet Union has not once complained about Germany's compliance with the terms of the treaty. Despite these unassailable truths and Germany's commitment to peace, the Reich finds itself at war with the Soviet Union.

"The Führer has assured me our response has been quick and decisive. Our invincible panzers (tanks) have crossed the Nieman River and even now are driving into Bolshevik territory. Luftwaffe has already dealt crippling blows to Soviet industry, communication and transportation, and to the Red Army itself. The Führer's generals at the front report German troops—your husbands, sons and brothers are being welcomed as liberators and heroes by those citizens who have long endured Soviet tyranny. Our military commanders predict that Moscow will fall within nine weeks.

"Sons and daughters of Germany, as we rally even more closely around the National Socialist Party and our great leader Adolf Hitler, we may know our enemies will be crushed and victory will be ours, because our cause is just." The speakers popped again and died. Silence swallowed the town.

Within minutes of the announcement, residents began to trickle into the streets of Hummelstadt. Trickles of citizens met and became streams, which surged into a river rushing violently toward the bank.

Juergen, who had been playing soccer with his friends Folker and Gerard not a block away from the epicenter of the public announcement, stood on the shore of the loud, rushing river. They watched it diverge at the square as men hurried to the bank and women headed for the grocery stores.

"Can you believe it?" Another soccer player, Franz whistled, lifted the soccer ball with his foot and bumped it over to Juergen, who caught it.

"Sure, I can believe our troops are advancing toward Moscow," Juergen replied, tucking the ball under his arm.

The lines soon formed at the bank tellers' windows and spilled out into the street. Men began to wave their worn checkbooks above their heads, demanding every Mark in their account.

"I'm going to tell my mother to get her money out of the bank while it still has some," Gerard said. He ran across the square and disappeared into the crowd.

Juergen and Folker kicked the ball back and forth in a side street off of the plaza for a while. The crowd in the clearing behind Juergen grew louder and more disorderly. By three o'clock it was clear the bank had closed. Soon, there was not a man who wasn't pushing his way toward the bank, shouting impatiently for his money.

Distant sirens grew closer as the police rushed to the scene. The police closed off all of the streets leading to the plaza, cleared the bank, and drove the mob away from the building. The two boys watched this excitement from behind a barricade that had been thrown up by nervous policemen. As the indignant crowd grew rowdier, one of the officers at the barricade approached the boys. "Why don't you two go home?" he asked them.

The two boys turned and headed down the street. They turned a corner and Juergen suggested they try and see what they could from the fifth floor windows of the Breitkopf mansion. Folker, however, decided it was probably time for him to go home and see how his family took the news. Juergen headed home alone, circumnavigating the plaza at a block's distance.

The banks remained closed for six days. When they reopened, the government had imposed a personal limit on withdrawals: two hundred Marks a month. This, however, did not have much of an impact on our family's resources. Mother had long since transferred all of her accounts to the local bank, and, bit by bit over several months, withdrawn a good deal of money and converted it into gold Krugerrands, a South African currency which would retain its value. She kept the bulk of the gold hidden in the yard and had not told anyone about it.

***

Erica and I hovered over the puzzle pieces spilled across the kitchen floor. Erica was working on the easy pieces—the pieces at the edge, the straight lines of Snow White's blue dress. I waited patiently. My sister would tire of the puzzle once she had completed the easier parts.

Just as Erica began to grumble and toss pieces down impatiently, Mother entered carrying the mail. We knew something was wrong when the handful of envelopes that she flung on the table overshot their mark and dropped to the floor. I looked down at the incomplete puzzle of the terrified maiden lost in the woods as Mother tore into an envelope. She muttered angrily to herself, slapped the letter onto the counter and turned to me. "Monica, get Hedwig. I need her right now." As I hurried from the room, I saw her hunched over the table scowling at the letter.

Hedwig was on the second floor, fluffing the goose-down pillows on my mother's bed. Today she was wearing my favorite outfit of hers, a transparent, sea green, floor length dress with large purple flowers. I watched Hedwig work for a moment before I addressed her. "Hedwig, mother wants to see you right away. She's angry."

"Oh, Monica, what have you done now?"

"She's not mad at us. It's the mail."

Hedwig smoothed the pillow she was holding and placed it on the bed. I followed her into the kitchen where we found Mother glaring at a smashed sheet of paper. Erica was still frowning at the puzzle.

"Just look at this!" Mother exclaimed, flattening the crumpled letter. "Six hundred grams of bread per day for an adult--that's not even a pound! Four hundred grams for dependents and children. Juergen could eat all of that in a single sitting. Three pounds of meat for an entire month! Only three pounds of cereal were available for a month. A pound and a half of fat. Five pounds of sugar or candy." Her voice rose with each item until she was too frustrated to continue.

Hedwig placed her hand on Mother's shoulder. "But, Frau Doctor, surely you can buy more."

"How? After the first of the month, the Mark will be useless for buying food." Mother paused. "I'm sending you down to the Provost's office with this." She handed Hedwig a blank form.

"What is it?" she asked.

"It's a petition for more ration cards. Tell them that you are married to Otto and he is in Belgium. That will make you the head of a household and entitle you to a proper ration allotment."

"But Otto already has a wife," Hedwig protested. "They won't believe me."

"Don't worry, Hedwig. I've been down there and none of the clerks are local. They won't know. How many Otto's do you think are in Belgium, anyway? And besides, there is going to be a line five blocks long down there today and every single person in it will be out for blood. You'll get your cards."

Hedwig was unconvinced. "They have records, Frau Doctor. They'll want an address."

"Tell them your address is twenty eight B ; you and your husband live in the shed." Mother bit her lip and then nodded her head. "Better yet, don't go to the Provost's office until a little later this afternoon. By then they'll be exhausted and will stamp anything to get rid of a screaming woman."

In the spring of 1942, a number of rations were cut, and the black market expanded. In winter of 1943-1944, the rations were officially set at barely an adequate level.

***

It was night and the rest of the household slept. I was in bed under my heavy comforter, which was more like an immense down pillow than a blanket. Although, it was spring, it still got very cold at night because Erica would not even attempt to go to sleep unless our window was cracked open. Hedwig buried us deeply beneath several layers of blankets before she turned out our light. I never had trouble falling asleep and was an unusually sound sleeper.

I was deep in a dream when I was shoved awake by Erica. I whined a little, but she shushed me. I barely resisted as she reached at my covers and pulled most of them to the floor, exposing my bare legs to the chilly air and shocking me awake. I wiggled and tugged down my nightgown, which was bunched up at the waist. I was about to pull my legs inside when Erica started to shake me, telling me to get out of bed and be quiet.

In her whole life, I don't think my sister ever slept more than three hours at a time. She was a restless little girl, forever waking to use the bathroom or finding some reason to go downstairs. Sometimes she would even put on a dress and shoes and go outside in the orchard behind the mansion. Occasionally, she woke me up, too, and took me along on her excursions. I only remember her getting caught outside once, when one of our staff unknowingly locked the door behind her. She circled the mansion in the dark for almost an hour, crying and retrying all the doors before pounding on the front door, calling for Hedwig. Father opened the door to his sobbing, terrified daughter and led her back to bed without asking any questions. When she realized she was not going to be discipled on the spot, she calmed down. He brought her back to our room, tucked her in, whispered, "Go to sleep, Erica," softly in her ear, and left without another word.

The next morning, it looked as if Erica was not going to be punished for sneaking out. Mother only greeted her at the table with a short, "I hope you enjoyed your little adventure last night." Erica did not answer and did not raise her eyes.

By the end of the school day, however, she had grown confident that she was forgiven and even bragged about it to me during our walk home from school. On the steps in front of the mansion, we met Hedwig, who took Erica by her hand and spanked her for Mother.

Erica tugged at my arm until I sat up in bed, my eyes bunched and blurry. "Stand up," she ordered, and too tired to resist, I did. When she was satisfied I was not going to crawl back into bed, she told me to follow her downstairs. As she sneaked out our bedroom door and disappeared in the hall, I noticed she was still wearing her nightgown and knew she was not planning to take me outside. I followed her down the hall and downstairs to the kitchen. Erica, ever stealthy, glanced around the room before she stepped inside. She crossed the room and beckoned me into the pantry.

"I'm not hungry," I told her, hoping she would let me go back to bed.

"No, come here," she hissed impatiently. She turned into the pantry, and as I approached, I heard the rustling of paper bags and jars being pushed around the shelves. I stood in the door of the pantry and watched my sister pull an entire loaf of bread from the paper bag the maids had brought home.

"Here," she said holding it out to me.

"I'm not hungry," I repeated, taking the long loaf in my arms.

"It is not for you," Erica said as she rummaged the shelves. I watched my sister for a moment as she gathered what I thought were going to be the ingredients of a very unappetizing sandwich. I laid the bread on the kitchen table next to the items she pulled out of the pantry: a bag of white sugar and a carton of cottage cheese. Then Erica opened a drawer, took out a knife and spoon, and sat next to me.

"What are you doing?" I asked.

"Making some bread for the stork," she replied matter-of-factly, opening the carton of cottage cheese and spooning dollops of it onto the bread. She then licked the spoon and started to sprinkle spoonfuls of sugar on top of the cottage cheese.

"What stork?"

"The stork that brings babies." She picked up the bread and carried them to one of the big windows in the kitchen, which she told me to open. I pulled on the handle and it swung open. There were two panes of glass between the kitchen and the outside; Erica laid an entire loaf of soggy bread between them and closed the window back up.

She told me to help her clean up, which I did, still not comprehending what she had done. I asked her again, and she finally gave me full explanation.

"At school Helga was talking about wanting a little sister. She said if you put bread with cottage cheese and sugar on it in the window, the stork will bring you a baby."

I hadn't ever wanted a little brother or sister before. Then again, I don't think the possibility had ever occurred to me.

***

In her youth, Frau Hirsch had been a vivacious debutante who married well enough to live in Bad Dekova with her wealthy husband. There, they became close friends of the Foersters, a modestly wealthy family who lived in Hummelstadt and attended our church. The

Hirsch's lived happily together for nearly fifty years and everybody was stunned, when in 1937, her husband took his life.

Frau Hirsch never fully recovered from the shock. A few months after her husband's death, Frau Hirsch sold the mansion in Bad Dekova and moved into a second-story residence along the main road in downtown Hummelstadt to be near the Foersters. Soon thereafter, she began to give away all of her possessions, and rumors began to spread that she was convinced it was the only way to save her husband's soul.

Over the years, her personality changed, too, and she drifted between states of mere eccentricity and feverish delirium. She bankrupted herself and increasingly depended on the charity of others during the war. Somehow, she alienated herself from the Foersters. Soon after, word arrived that the Russians had stopped the German advance in the East. The Foersters disappeared, presumably to the West. Frau Hirsch was alone.

Unfortunately, I am unable provide an accurate physical description of Frau Hirsch. To my knowledge, I never met her. Likewise, neither my mother nor Hedwig was able to summon an image of Frau Hirsch's face when asked. Both of them, however, relayed the only impression that remained of her, in my mother's words, "I don't think she was very big."

Bankrupt and abandoned, Frau Hirsch was taken in by Herr Piehl, who gave her a bed in a spare room above the Gasthaus. Even though she never came down while I was at the restaurant, I confirmed she did live above the main dining room.

One morning, I woke up early enough to accompany Hedwig to town to pick up our ration of bread and passed Herr Piehl's Gasthaus on the way to the bakery. That morning, he was sweeping the sidewalk before putting out the tables. He spotted us and waved. "Hedwig!" he shouted, "Come here! I want to show you something. Hello, Fräulein Breitkopf. How are you this morning? You are looking very pretty today. Bosel will want to know you are here. Now, Hedwig, I know you will appreciate this. You cook, don't you?" He was clearly very excited, and I had the impression that he hadn't really been sweeping, but was merely pretending so he could pull us off the street to show off the whatever-it was he had called Hedwig to see.

He invited us into the empty restaurant. Inside, I immediately started looking for Bosel while Hedwig followed Herr Piehl into the kitchen. The familiar room looked and sounded different in the morning. The chairs had been turned upside-down on the edges of the tables, which made the dining room look like a hall full of enormous insects stranded on their backs, making it difficult for me to see if Bosel was in the room. I crept around the tables partly to avoid startling Bosel and partly to avoid startling myself. It was while I was searching that I heard Frau Hirsch.

The ceiling creaked directly above my head and I held perfectly still. The floorboards squeaked beneath her feet as she slowly walked the length of the dining room, paused, and walked back. She walked back and forth and back and forth for five full minutes. I stood listening, imagining what Frau Hirsch looked like. My imagination substituted a terrifying image for a realistic one. I imagined her bent back, with thin, spotty arms, in a long white nightgown, wearing pale blue slippers and a wrinkled face.

I think I would have run if an unseen hand hadn't pushed open the kitchen door and I hadn't heard the click-click-click of toenails on wood. I turned to see Bosel's fur swishing behind the legs of the tables.

Bosel thrust his snout impatiently into my hand and took a step forward as if to show me exactly how to properly pet him. I ran my hand back and forth through his shaggy mane and along the thick, flat coat on his back. I kissed the top of his head and he gave me big wet kisses all over my face. "Bosel, don't," I giggled, looking away and rubbing his cheeks the best I could without looking. Bosel tickled everything from my throat to my nose with his tongue and I fell to the floor laughing. I covered the back of my neck with my hands in case he wanted to lick it. Bosel flopped on the floor beside me so my hands would be within scratching distance. I rubbed up and down his back and he rolled over onto his side. I buried my nose in his fur and pulled myself over so I could rest my head on him. My arms stretched across Bosel's body and I put my cheek to his side. I could hear Bosel's breath and his quick heartbeat as I was soothed by the steady rising and falling of his chest. I had forgotten all about Frau Hirsch.

We were still on the floor when Herr Piehl and Hedwig emerged from the kitchen.

"Well, it's very nice, Herr Piehl," Hedwig remarked sincerely. "I've certainly never seen such a big oven before."

"Thank you, Hedwig. I knew you would appreciate it. It will be useful when the war is over and the soldiers return." He looked around. "Now, where is Monica?" he asked, but I knew he had seen me. I pretended to sleep as he tiptoed across the room. "I think she's asleep!" he said.

"She was up very early this morning." Hedwig did not tiptoe over to me, but before she reached me, Herr Piehl diplomatically offered, "Hedwig, why don't you finish your errands while Bosel and I stay with her?"

Hedwig agreed and told Herr Piehl when she would return. When she had gone, I pretended to wake up, rubbing my eyes. "Good morning, Fraulein Breitkopf. I hope you slept well." I smiled, hugged Bosel, and stood up. Herr Piehl offered me his hand. "Do you want to see what I showed to Hedwig?"

I shrugged, and as we were walking toward the kitchen I asked, "What is it?"

"Oh, you'll love it. Come here, Bosel." The dog rolled over onto its feet and followed us.

***

The siren went off at the center of town at 11:00 p.m., long after we had been sent to bed. I vaguely knew what the siren meant, but I was not yet awake. Erica showed no intention of getting up and seemed to sleep peacefully. I sat up and tried to remember what the siren meant and if I was supposed to wake Erica. Then, Hedwig rushed in and told us to hurry down to the kitchen as fast as we could. I felt my way to the grand staircase, where I met my mother. She took my hand and told me to stay with her. "Where's your sister?" she asked, but I didn't know. Just then, I heard Erica sobbing in the hall behind us as Hedwig carried her toward the kitchen. Erica did not want to wake up and threw a tiny, fussy tantrum in the dark. Mother told Hedwig to take us to the kitchen and stay with us.

Juergen was already waiting for us by the time we reached the kitchen. Unlike me, he instantly knew what the sirens meant—he learned all about them in the Hitlerjugend.

One day after school, he had asked mother if we had a plan for the mansion in case of an air raid. He helped her decide on the kitchen as our shelter and placed an air raid kit under the sink in case the house was damaged in an attack.

Hedwig set my sister down in a chair at the table, and Erica immediately slumped over the tabletop and buried her eyes in her folded arms. I covered my eyes and reached for the light switch. As soon as the lights turned on, Juergen raced across the room, knocked my hand away, and turned them off. "What do you want to do" he hissed in my face, "tell them where we are?"

"Who?"

"The enemy! They'll see our house from their planes and drop bombs on us."

"We have the black curtains up," I argued.

"You don't want to take chances. What if there is a hole in one of them? Then we're telling them where we are. Stay away from the lights," he ordered. He stood as if at attention and made it clear that he was now guarding the lights. I sat down at the table.

A minute passed. I listened to the wail of the siren. Then Erica began sobbing again. "Where's mama?" she asked. I realized mother was still in the mansion. I was suddenly very afraid, even when I heard Hedwig say, "She's coming. It's alright." Hedwig rubbed Erica's back and started to pray softly.

A moment later, mother and Herr Thienelt came through the door, each carrying a bundle of bed sheets and pillows. "Is everyone here?" Mother dropped the sheets she was carrying and asked Hedwig to spread them out on the floor for us.

Mother picked Erica up and tucked her into a nest of pillows and sheets. I sat down on another. My family sat silently in the dark. Faintly at first, but steadily louder, a new sound came through the walls on all sides and filled the room.

"Airplanes," Juergen whispered excitedly. We had heard and saw many military planes overhead since the beginning of the war, but this was the first time they were not German warplanes. Juergen, who sat on the floor underneath the light switch, hopped up and ran to one of the kitchen's large windows. He pulled back one corner of the curtain to look out. When the moonlight fell on mother's eye, she hurried to the window and snatched the curtain away from my brother. "Juergen!" she snapped, smacking him on the backside. "Never do that again!"

"But I need to see what kind they are, mama."

"I don't care. We are keeping the curtains closed." Mother's voice was stern and Juergen could not argue.

"Would they tell us on the radio?"

"You can turn it on, but softly, so your sisters can sleep."

Sleep for me, however, was out of the question. There was too much happening: Hedwig praying, the loud sirens, Erica sobbing in her sleep, the radio announcer talking, loud enough to hear but not loud enough to understand, the warm, heavy, air locked in with us, and above and behind it all, the searching planes.

The bombers passed overhead unchallenged for hours, it seemed. I crawled into a bundle of blankets on the floor next to Juergen and listened to the radio. I lay there stiffly, unwilling to move. I was so nervous my muscles started to ache after a while, and I was sweating into my pillow. Finally, I kicked away the blanket, but the air in the room was no less stifling.

"They are heading for a big city," Juergen reported to mother and Herr Thienelt. "Breslau or someplace like that. I'm glad we live in the country, but I wish we could shoot at them."

Herr Thienelt got up from the table and pulled his chair nearer to the radio, where he sat and listened intently. Mother, who had been sitting across from him, followed him wordlessly and pulled her chair next to his. They sat there silently together all night, their faces softly illuminated by the only light in the whole house, the glowing face of the radio. Occasionally, they exchanged nervous glances with one another, and, recognizing their own nervousness in the other's eyes, they took comfort in knowing they were not alone.

Listening to the announcer's report of enemy planes over Germany was strangely like listening to a weather forecast: a wave of bombers over Silesia, one to the north heading north and the announcer's list of towns whose citizens should take shelter from the coming storm. We were promised we were meeting the bombers head on, but we heard no explosions, no anti-aircraft fire, nor anything else to suggest the vast cloud of enemy planes was meeting any resistance. As the hours wore on and the planes proceeded unabated, I was afraid if all of those planes dropped their bombs on German cities, eventually there would be nothing left to bomb and small country towns like Hummelstadt would be next.

That night, and on many nights thereafter, the whole world collapsed into the size of our kitchen, the limit of all things good. Everything beyond was forbidden, dangerous and evil.

∗∗∗

Not long after the first air raid, Hedwig noticed something missing from one of the parlors. Her first thought was the pillow had been mistakenly placed on another couch, so she checked on the couches, but it wasn't there. She then asked Anneliese to keep her eyes open. In a few days, both maids suspended all other housework to thoroughly search the entire mansion for the pillow. They found nothing.

In most homes, I imagine, a missing pillow would probably not be a cause of so much concern. Not in my mother's home. Most of the furniture in our house was expensive and not only served functional purposes, but considered one-of-a-kind pieces and works of art. They doubled as conversation pieces. Each was my mother's prized possession. The hand-painted silk pillow had been a wedding present. The sense of urgency the loss of the pillow inspired in the maids was augmented by Hedwig's acute sense of responsibility to my mother, and the unnatural attention to order which she brought to her job. She was, therefore, very near tears when she reported to my mother that the pillow had been missing for over a week.

Mother was not overly concerned, but that night at dinner, she asked everyone in the household if we had seen the pillow or moved it. I said I hadn't, which was the truth. Erica said she would help Hedwig look for it after we had eaten. Juergen was disinterested in the pillow, but thought it wise to make known his ignorance of the pillow's whereabouts in front of everyone else. Nobody suspected Mr. Thienelt. As far as we were concerned, he was as trustworthy as Hedwig.

In time, we accepted the pillow's mysterious disappearance would never be explained. In fact, it was only weeks later when nobody was looking for it, that it resurfaced. Juergen found it while he was playing in the backyard. He brought the soiled, soggy pillow to mother, who asked him where it had been.

"I found it in the chicken coop. Someone hid it just inside the door where nobody could see it."

Suspecting one of us would be able to fill in the missing details, she summoned Erica and me to the kitchen for questioning. When Erica saw the pillow, she blushed nervously and confessed.

After the first air raid, Erica realized her pets, the fancy chickens we kept in the yard, were not protected during the air raid. Thinking the mansion's heavy blackout curtains were for keeping the bombs out, she had gone to the backyard every night before bed and barricaded the door of the chicken coop so the chickens would be safe. Now that she had been found out, Erica was terrified of the spanking she expected to receive.

Mother did not have Erica spanked. In fact, she did not even scold her. As she listened to her daughter's story, mother's stern face gradually brightened. By the time Erica finished, Mother was laughing hysterically and trying to catch her breath. It was, I think, the first real laugh my mother had since the air raids began, and her face turned quite red. She could only manage a breathless "Oh, then!" before bursting into another laugh. When she finally managed to catch her breath again, she gave both of us hugs and kissed Erica on the cheek. She smiled at Erica fondly, wiped her eyes, and gently asked her not to do it again. She then took the ruined pillow and left the room to tell Herr Thienelt about the pillow's discovery.

Several days had passed before Erica and I realized Martha was gone. It came out during a fight between Erica and Juergen, in which Juergen ended the fight by daring Erica to ask mother what had happened to Martha. Erica immediately stormed downstairs, where she found mother in the pantry taking inventory of the rations. "Where's

Martha?" she asked sternly.

Mother was accustomed to Erica's tendency to materialize suddenly when angry. She was not in the least intimidated by Erica's challenge. She turned to face her daughter and asked, "Who do you think you are talking to, young lady? You don't talk to anyone like that. Ask again, politely."

This frustrated Erica further, but mother's intolerance of Erica's temper was one of the few things that could make my sister behave. "Mother," she said in a lower tone, "What happened to Martha?"

Mother placed the list she was making on a shelf and told Erica to go upstairs and bring me down to the kitchen. When we returned, mother was sitting at the table and the radio was turned off. Erica sat across from her and I sat next to her.

"Monica," mother began, "Erica asked me where Martha is, and I wanted you to hear my answer, too." I was confused, but I nodded because my mother had a serious look on her face. Erica looked cross. "Martha is not here because she does not work here anymore."

This was the first time I had noticed Martha was missing, and for a second I thought I had not understood what my mother had said. I could not imagine what I had heard.

"Martha broke one of the rules of the house, and I asked her to leave and she agreed."

"Can she ever come back?" asked Erica.

Mother shook her head.

"Where is she now?" I asked.

Mother didn't answer. She did not know. I was stunned and hurt and started to cry. Erica glared at the floor and asked, "What did she do?"

"Like I said, she broke a rule. It wasn't the first time, and she knew she couldn't break any more. But she decided it was more important to break the rule than work here."

Of course, that explanation was completely unsatisfying, but when I later learned what her offense had been, I don't think I would have completely understood.

Martha, who was a little younger than my mother, had recently taken to dating questionable younger men and had become accustomed to going out after the rest of the household went to bed. Of course, she was exhausted the next day and of little use to anyone. This frustrated all of her coworkers, not to mention her employer. Mother had spoken with her about how her social life was interfering with her work and insisted that it stop. Apparently, Martha thought she would be more awake in the morning if she brought her boyfriends home to sleep. Mother had caught them and Martha's fate was sealed. She left the next day while we were at school.

Mother felt the slightest indiscretion, if discovered by the wrong person, could make life more difficult than it already was becoming for the family. At any rate, mother already had three children and a house to take care of without Martha to worry about. She knew Martha would have a difficult time getting another job, at least one that was not related to the war industry, so she advanced her several months pay in Krugerrands, which were still worth something.

**

"Left flank, march!"

The soldiers stepped in unison and made a crisply executed turn.

"Right flank, march!" the ranking officer shouted, and the entire column adjusted without skipping a beat. They kicked their feet out straight and high in front of them and brought them down in lockstep.

"To the rear, march!" "Column left, march!"

The officer brought his soldiers to a halt and began his inspection, slowly working his way down the line, checking every crease and button on the soldiers' uniforms. Before taking his position at the end of the line, he took each soldier's weapon and inspected it. When the officer was satisfied, the prisoner was led out of the holding cell and presented to the firing squad. He was a high-ranking government official, and he strutted slowly and proudly, as if to suggest he was, in fact, in charge of his fate.

"Dickus Huhn, you have been sentenced to death by firing squad for the crimes of treason, conspiracy, espionage and sabotage." The prisoner did not seem to be paying attention to the proceedings, and having refused a blindfold, cast his eyes about the courtyard before finally fixing them on the ground.

The firing squad loaded their weapons, each soldier slid a single shell into his rifle and awaited the commander's signal. The officer raised his ceremonial sword and brought it down sharply: "Fire!" The rifles kicked back, and the prisoner flopped on the ground.

I was anxiously watching the execution from a window on the third floor of the mansion. "Erica!" I shouted. "They shot Dickus! I think he's hurt!" Sobbing heavily, I hurried for the door.

Erica stood at the door. Her arms were crossed and her eyes were rolling. "Don't be so stupid, Monica," she said condescendingly. "The boys are just playing. Dickus is fine."

"But they shot him! I saw it! He looked hurt!"

Erica shook her head, and looking very much like Hedwig, I thought, tossed out her palms in frustration and stared at the ceiling. To prove her point, Erica grabbed my sleeve and dragged me to the window. "See?"

In the yard below, the boys stood at attention in the firing line. Dickus, the chicken, who had been startled by Juergen's command to fire, settled down and was pecking at the ground, showing little further interest in the boys' game. I, however, could not be consoled until I ran into the yard and was assured our pet was unharmed.

I later learned that mother and Hedwig had watched the execution in the yard from the second floor.

"Where are the girls?" mother asked.

"They're in their room, Frau Doctor." She paused. "The boys really do think they're soldiers, don't they?"

"They are——they're Hitlerjugend.

The boys in my neighborhood played war when I was a little girl, but they didn't know anything about marching or orders or guns. "Our children can outrank one another. Do you know the other boys?"

"The youngest one, the one without a uniform, is Helga Keitel's brother Franz. He wants to be Schutzstaffel (SS)." Mother made no response. "I'm not sure whether or not Juergen wants to be, but sometimes he acts like it," Hedwig mused.

Steps sounded in the hallway as I rushed down the stairs with

Erica. Mother said, "Herr Keitel has told me he'd rather the boy be dead than see him in the SS, Hedwig." Mother had similar thoughts about Juergen. "But we have time. Juergen is only ten. He can't join until he's eighteen."

Mother looked stern as we ran across the yard to the chicken. I was still crying. "Do you see how they frightened Monica?" mother asked. "They're learning to intimidate people with violence. Right now, they are using sticks to execute chickens, but one day they will be given guns to shoot people. I hope I never see that day." The boys began to march around the yard again.

"They may lower the age if the war does not go well."

"Well, even if they lowered the age to sixteen, we would still have six years. But the boys will have learned so much by then. I'm afraid if the Führer outlasts the war, by the time the boys are old enough to become SS, we may have lost them."

The two women stood together at the window and watched Juergen bring the column to a halt and dismiss his troops. The column dispersed and the boys piled into the shed, their hideout. Erica and I crouched by the chicken coop and peered inside. My mother touched Hedwig's arm and squeezed gently. "Dear, would you go out and keep an eye on the girls? I trust Juergen, but I don't like the twins being out alone anymore."

Hedwig left without another word. It was understood that mother would stand at the window and watch over her children from above.

***

That evening, after an unsatisfying dinner, which consisted of a thin, flour soup Hedwig cooked for us, Erica and I retired to our room. At dinner, mother had been tired and grumpy. Dinner had been late, so we were sent to bed shortly after the meal. We girls with grumbling tummies were not content to sleep. Hedwig followed us around outside that afternoon, and even though we loved Hedwig, we decided to stay awake in our beds until we could sneak outside by ourselves. We passed the time planning our escape in whispers, determined to have a proper adventure.

"Do you know where the flashlight is?"
"No, but I think there are candles and matches in the shed."
"What if we can't find any?"
"Any what?"
"Candles or matches."
"Well, if there are no candles, then we can use the lantern."
"I don't think we should use it. Mama was angry with Anneliese the other night when she kicked over the lantern on accident. She was telling her how expensive the oil was and how hard it was to get."
"Then we'll use the moon."
"But I don't want to go outside in the dark."
"I don't care. I want to see what the boys are hiding in the shed they don't want us to see."
"Me, too."
"What do you think they have in there?"
"Secrets."
"What type of secrets?"
"I don't know. They didn't tell me."
"I hope there is some food for Dickus in there."

We crept downstairs into the yard, and opened the shed door very slightly and slipped in. Like most windows in Germany, the shed window was covered by a thick black cloth to shield light from enemy bombers in case of an air raid. Erica felt her way along the wall and pulled the curtain away from the window. Moonlight crept in.

Juergen and his companions converted the shed into a military headquarters. A poster of Wehrmacht soldiers marching in rows in front of German airplanes had been hung on the wall. A battered table, which neither of us had seen before, filled the center of the room and was encircled by wooden crates turned on their sides. In one corner, the boys had placed a large footlocker. Next to it, the sticks that substituted as guns that afternoon leaned against the wall in a neat line. Erica approached the footlocker and opened it, but she could not see inside. She reached in and pulled out a notebook with Juergen's name scrawled on it. "Look, Monica!" she hissed. "I found Juergen's diary."

The notebook was more of a homework book from the Hitlerjugend than a diary. Earlier in the war, Juergen carried the book with him at all times, and even in the dim light of the moon, we recognized its cover. He kept a record of what he did in the Hitlerjugend and what he read or heard about the war. He spent a lot of time praising Germany's soldiers, spilling his pure admiration for them onto paper. In the margins, he had drawn tanks and airplanes. We weren't surprised by this. Juergen spent most of his free time engrossed by the war, as if it was a hobby. It seemed he was trying to convince Erica and me to take it up, too.

Erica moaned. "I don't want to read any more about the war; the war is boring." She placed the diary on the table while I dipped into the mysterious box. I felt like a magician when I pulled out three chocolate bars wrapped in paper.

"Erica! Look at this! Chocolate!"

Erica put her nose close to my outstretched hands, squinted and began to empty the box of its contents. By the time the box had been emptied, the notebook was buried under a pile of chocolate, hard candy, small bags of peanuts, two small loaves of hard bread, a package of partly melted butter and three oranges. We, for an instant, were amazed with our luck. "Where did Juergen get all of this?" I wondered aloud.

Erica shrugged, "He probably went into the pantry and stole it."

"Should we tell Hedwig?"

Erica shook her head. "No, he probably gives it to the other boys."

"But if it's ours, we should get to eat it and not Juergen's friends. We can't get any more and I'm hungry."

I eyed the pile of treats longingly. I almost agreed with her; maybe we were not as hungry or as skinny as many of Juergen's friends. She noticed it this morning after they rushed out into the yard. Franz's face seemed smaller, his cheeks appeared somehow sharper, and his eyes had sunk a little deeper into his head. It was strange and scary, and you could see his bones. "No, we can't tell," Erica decided. "Some of Juergen's friends are even hungrier than we are."

I sighed, but broke a hunk of chocolate off one of the bars anyway and gave half of it to my sister. When we had eaten, I began to clear off the table. Erica closed the curtain and we slipped out into the night.

Uncertain Flight

***

One afternoon in the spring of 1944, I saw something that caused my mother to ban us from playing outside without supervision. I was sitting on one of the fifth-floor balconies overlooking Hummelstadt. The sun was beginning to set and birds were chirping in the trees below.

The balcony was a favorite place of mine, since I could play with my dolls there without interruption. Together, we spied on the town, looked into backyards, surveyed the streets and kept an eye out for people I knew. I watched women go into the stores, the traffic on the sidewalks, and my father's clients coming to his law office.

On this evening, however, I witnessed a man being arrested by the Gestapo. (Nazi) It hardly meant a thing to me when I watched it. At that age, I was not conscious of the turmoil around me. Only later that night, at dinner, when one of the maids reported that Herr Kampfel, a neighbor down the street, had been arrested, did I consider what I had seen was any way out of the ordinary. I was merely excited that I had a story that interested the adults intensely.

I did not know Herr Kampfel at all, and that meal was the only time that my family talked about him. I told them I had been on the balcony when I saw two cars pull up next to the house on the corner. Four uniformed men jumped out of the first car. Two of them hurried around to the back of the house while the other two proceeded to the front door. In a moment, the front door opened and one of the men went inside. When he emerged, he was escorting an old man with white hair, who walked quickly to the first car. The men who went around to the back came out, and one of them climbed into the second car while the rest sat with the man in the first car. The small motorcade pulled away much more quickly than it had arrived and sped toward the Provost's office.

In retrospect, I now suspect the men who went around the back were there in case the man tried to escape. If you had seen the old man's stoop and shuffle, there was no way he could have fled.

Everyone at the table listened to my story intently, and I made the most of my moment in the spotlight. Herr Thienelt and my mother looked worried. After dinner, when I told Hedwig what I had seen, she reacted the same way.

The next morning, mother insisted on walking Erica and me to school. Before we left, she gave us a stern lecture in the hallway, and her eyes were so earnest, even Erica seemed to take her words to heart. "From now on," mother said, "I don't want you two walking home from school alone. You wait there until someone comes to pick you up. It will be either me or Hedwig, and I don't want you to step off of the playground until we get there. This is from now on. Do you understand?"

Erica and I nodded.

Mother looked at us sternly for a moment to make sure she had made her point.

"Good girls," she praised out loud. "One more thing," she added, looking at me.

"Monica, I don't want you to tell anyone about what you saw last night. It's none of our business, and I feel bad we talked about it at dinner. Don't tell your classmates, don't tell Helga, don't even tell your teacher. It's none of their business either, and it's not nice to spread rumors. And it's none of your business, Erica, so you forget about it, too."

After that, things at home changed for us. We were not allowed to play at our friends' houses. Even Jeurgen found himself at home more often. After the arrest, mother insisted we invite our friends over to play, and the sedate rhythm of living in our mansion had changed.

The former pulse of our house was gone. We twins, still at such a young age, heard words and phrases we didn't understand. We heard anger, fear, and terror from the radio, even though we were not allowed to listen to national broadcasting. Our mother dismissed our questions and told us to pay no attention, and she instructed the maids to tell us nothing.

Our older brother Juergen, by three years, delighted in his role as senior adviser, who amplified and embroidered the graphics of his version of the beginning months of World War II. He drew us into the war, by showing us incomprehensible maps and pretending to be a soldier. He pointed out cities to us, and we picked up the excitement from him. We learned about Rotterdam, Belgium and the Maginot Line. We learned new words like "Blitzkrieg" that became our definition of the war. The lightening described the German sweep of Poland. The rest of the war was not lightening. It dragged on and on, and soon our panic of the first two weeks, the daily radio broadcasts describing the German advance into the low country to the west, became monotonous. In the daily broadcasts, we heard of thousands being killed and tens of thousands losing their homes.

***

The Nazi regime became a devastating, traumatic, heart-wrenching, life-altering experience. The war caused the German people great suffering, hardship, economic wounds, and much distress. People were deported, sent to jail, and never heard from again. One wrong word could get you reported to the police station.

You could recognize a Nazi right away by their dark uniform. I have often wondered if they didn't sleep in it. Some of the Nazis were very ordinary, simple people, who had little or no education. Being a Nazi made them feel very important, and they also had a chance to get a better paying job. Often at night, you could hear them getting drunk and being very noisy, as they often stood at street corners smoking cigarettes.

There was this one Nazi. He showed up in our church one Sunday morning. He was sitting in the back of the church. Of course, everyone in church noticed him right away, and many people felt very uneasy around him. Why shouldn't they be? He was in his Nazi uniform, wearing shiny, polished shoes. His black Mercedes was parked outside in front of the church and noticed by everyone.

***

After the church service this Sunday, we heard unusually loud talking with the pastor, in the back of the room, where people gathered after church for coffee and cookies. The conversation between those two people became louder and louder. It was obvious the Nazi had been drinking. Everyone became nervous and feared for the worst.

We found out our pastor mentioned something in his sermon that this Nazi didn't want to hear, and he wanted to arrest the pastor. Our pastor was a very pleasant, nice man of God with a slow speaking voice. He was finally able to convince this officer, that he must have misunderstood him. The Nazi finally left the room and disappeared in his Mercedes. Everyone in church started breathing again. Of course, the people got very worried as we thought he would have been reported and we would never see our pastor again.

Once, my mother couldn't help saying something bad about Hitler. She was in the store with many people, so afraid, that somebody in the store could have heard it.

She even thought of leaving the mansion for a couple of weeks after that occasion, being so afraid of the Nazis. Fortunately, she was not reported to the police station. One wrong word could get you reported to the police station.

Usually, the people who were reported were picked up by the Nazis. They were only allowed a one or two day trial and after the trial, they were sent to camp or shot immediately.

Much later when the war was over, Hedwig was sitting in a train traveling to visit friends. She was surprised, because she recognized three well dressed gentlemen, who played a big role in Hummelstadt during the war. They sat directly opposite her in the same compartment. She was very sure that she recognized the three Nazis, who were always in uniform back in the war years. Hedwig hid her face behind a newspaper, pretending not to know them. Many Nazis shot themselves before the Russian army invaded our village. Hedwig knew about one Nazi couple who were found shot to death in a garden gazebo.

***

At the end of the summer, my mother found herself visiting the town Provost. His name was Captain Schimmel, and he was the highest-ranking Nazi official in the town. Mother had entertained the captain at the mansion on several occasions. Although she was friendly with him, she kept him at arm's length. Nonetheless, he became an admirer of mother's and, on occasion, had been able to provide her with extra rations and other small favors. He had even helped her rent an apartment in Berlin, since it was impossible for her to travel there to oversee the purchase herself.

This visit, however, was not social. That weekend, Hedwig had returned from her parents' house in Friedersdorf when she was attacked and robbed by three drunken boys in uniform. Hedwig had recognized two of them from the Provost's office. When Mother heard about it, she was furious and promised Hedwig that she would get her property back.

The Provost's waiting room smelled of furniture polish and tobacco smoke, and a clattering teletype punched away somewhere down the hallway. My mother gave her name to the young man in the SS uniform at the desk.

"Captain Schimmel is running on time this morning. He will see you shortly."

She took a seat on a wooden bench directly across from the boy in uniform. While she waited, he adjusted the small black electric fan on the desktop.

The clerk called mother and ushered her into the Provost's office. Captain Schimmel was sitting at his desk behind his nameplate. "Did you find them?" she asked.

"Yes," he said calmly. "What they did was inexcusable." He pulled a large envelope from his desk and handed it to mother. "Everything is there. Please apologize to Hedwig for me."

"Are they going to be punished?" Mother asked.

"They won't be court-martialed, but I had them transferred to fighting units. Also," he added, "I have taken the liberty to draw up traveling papers for your family. I felt I owed you a favor."

"I haven't traveled since the war started."

"These papers are almost impossible to get, Frau Breitkopf, and they're going to become much more valuable before long. I have seats for yourself, Hedwig, your son and your daughters. I will hold them for you, if you like. You only have to ask for them. I think you will find them indispensable." Mother thanked him, but said she was not yet willing to leave Hummelstadt. But in her thoughts she knew, that it had never crossed her mind to leave the mansion. I remember talking with her about it many times.

"Very well, I will hold them here."

In the last days before the Russians entered Hummelstadt, Mother returned to the Provost's office for the traveling papers, but the office had been closed. Captain Schimmel had fled.

Others who visited the Provost's office had different experiences. "What do you mean it's my fault?" the old woman sobbed. She trembled in anger and fear. Like everyone else in the line, she was thin and pale, her balance was somewhat wobbly, and her right hand was palsied. She could barely stand, and the trip to the Provost's office must have fatigued her greatly. "We have nothing left! Not even to sell!" The soldier made no reply——he was not even listening to her. The woman simply cried.

Mother watched from our place in the line. We could not move to comfort the woman or we would lose our place in the ration card line, and we had already been waiting for two hours. Our rations were meager, but in the last few weeks, mother had been giving a large portion of her daily allotment to us. She thought we had become frighteningly skinny and therefore had written to father for help. She also, like everyone else in the line, was looking to the Provost for assistance.

The old woman continued to argue at the uniformed clerk's desk:

"I haven't picked up our cards yet. I don't understand why you won't believe me."

The soldier held his clipboard close to her face and pointed to the signature next to her household name. She inspected it and burst into tears. "It's not even my signature or my husband's! He's too ill to get out of bed. Someone has signed there by mistake! Can't you read that?"

"I can't read it, madam. As far as we're concerned, it means that you have received your rations. Giving you two more sets of cards would be taking the food out of someone else's mouth. I don't have the authority to do that."

The woman looked shattered.

"We have no heat. We have no food. It's going to get cold soon. How can we survive without food?"

***

Christmas passed that winter without much gaiety. There were few presents and there was no tree, but the maids decorated one room for us to spend Christmas in. One of the few presents I got that year was a new dress for one of my dolls. Mother had cut up one of her old dresses to make it. I still have a letter that I wrote to my father about a month later.

January 31, 1945 Hummelstadt

Dear father,

We want to write you today. The Russians will arrive here very soon. We are all so afraid, dear father. Please come home and get us. We are very frightened. We want to be with you.

Two of our pet chickens died. They were so sick. Schobers is the only one left. We are left all alone in that big mansion. For Christmas I got a bag I can use when I go swimming. I also got some gloves for going out in the snow.

Your loving daughter,

Moni

***

Mother and Hedwig made the dreary trip from the mansion to the Gasthaus zur Krone. A freezing shroud of drifting snow painted the town gray. The sidewalks had not been cleared for weeks. The first snow only partially melted and had refrozen on the cobblestones, and a fresh layer of snow had fallen during the night. Most people did not leave their houses anymore unless they had to, especially during the cold weather. But mother had business to discuss with Herr Piehl that morning.

The women stepped around the body of an old man who had died sometime that morning on the footpath across from the Provost's office. Someone had rolled him onto his back and spread a bed sheet over him. All they could see of the man were his tall, rubber boots (the kind that were so difficult to find, according to Hedwig) and his left hand freezing on top of the snow.

On the next block, a dead horse was sprawled in the middle of the street. There were few able-bodied men left in town to remove the bodies, and it would be impossible to bury them in the frozen earth without heavy machinery. Those who otherwise might have volunteered to clear the corpses conserved what little energy their meager rations gave them. The citizens of Hummelstadt had silently agreed that the living could not afford to expend any resources on the dead.

Further ahead, mother and Hedwig spied another fresh corpse. It was that of an elderly woman in tattered clothing who had died on the sidewalk in front of the bakery. She was on her side, but her legs were sprawled out flat in a wide V. Her eyes were closed and her arms reached limply toward the two women. As mother and Hedwig started to step around the body, the corpse twitched and began to writhe pitifully. Hedwig yelped and nearly lost her footing when one arm thrashed against the side of her boot. My mother was startled too, but then she realized what had happened.

"Dear, angel, help me," the woman said helplessly. "Please don't leave. I can't get up on my own."

The woman's words prompted my mother to crouch over the woman and ask gently, "Did you break anything?"

"No, dear, I fell in the snow. I don't think anything is broken."

"Are you strong enough to stand?"

"Yes. Please help me up. I can stand on my own, but I slipped on the ice."

Hedwig, who had recovered enough from the shock of the woman's unexpected resurrection to ask her if she needed a doctor, struggled to regain her composure.

"No, I'll be fine," the woman replied.

Hedwig and my mother helped the trembling woman to her feet. Her white face stood out against her black hat and dark, ragged coat. Snow was sticking to her face, but the tears made tracks down her cheeks. Hedwig reached into her handbag and gave the woman her handkerchief—it was all she could think of to do. The woman thanked her, wiped her cheeks, blew her nose, and slipped the handkerchief into her coat pocket. Hedwig said nothing.

Mother bent down to collect the woman's handbag, the contents of which had spilled into the snow. She quickly dusted off what snow she could from each article before returning it to the purse. She returned the handbag to its owner, who quietly thanked them both. Then the woman turned and worked herself slowly toward the door of the bakery. Mother and Hedwig waited until the woman had her hand on the door before they continued.

"Poor woman," said Hedwig. "The old will be the first to die this winter." Mother said nothing. They had only gone a few meters before they heard the voice of the old woman calling out from behind them.

"Please help me! I can't find my bread card! Did you see it, ladies? I can't find it!"

For a moment, Mother considered turning to help the woman scour the ground for the card, but they walked on as if they hadn't heard her. She had seen no bread card as she repacked the old woman's purse, so she could not help her. The women turned at the next corner.

The snow crunched beneath their feet as they approached the Gasthaus zur Krone. Hedwig looked on while Mother knocked on the door. There was no answer. Hedwig rubbed some condensation off of the restaurant window and shielded her eyes with her mittens to peer inside. A single candle lay on a table next to the bar. Herr Piehl sat immobile, staring into the candle, lost in thought. He started to come to when Hedwig tapped on the pane.

Herr Piehl came to the door to let them in. Mother barely recognized her longtime friend. His cheeks had grown pale and gaunt from hunger, and his chin cast a deep, sharp shadow across his neck. His weary eyes, however, were as warm and soft and kind as they had ever been. The rest of his body was hidden by a bulky floor-length overcoat that was tied together in front around a very skinny waist. Hummelstadt was no longer receiving enough power to heat the houses except at night.

He straightened his wireless spectacles and smiled at them. "Frau

Breitkopf, Hedwig, it's very good to see you." He kissed each of them on the cheek, ushered them inside and locked the door behind him. "We don't get many visitors anymore," he remarked as he led them to a table near the bar. "May I ask what could possibly drag you down from the mansion on such an awful day?"

"We came here to visit you, Herr Piehl," Hedwig answered. "We haven't seen you for quite a while."

"I wanted to check in on your man Petersen," Mother added.

"Well, I apologize for being so scarce lately. Bosel and I have been very busy lately taking care of Frau Hirsch."

"How is Bosel, Herr Piehl?" my mother asked. "The children ask about him everyday."

Herr Piehl smiled.

"Please tell them that he is doing well and he has been asking when they are going to visit." Herr Piehl removed his gloves and placed them in his pocket. "Would you care for lunch? We have two specials today. The first is an excellent turnip soup served with black bread, or if you prefer, we have some black bread which is very nice and is served with a bowl of turnip soup. Do you need a moment to decide?"

My mother laughed, leaned against her armrest and looked up at Herr Piehl, who held an invisible pencil and scratch pad. "I'll have the turnip soup and black bread," she said.

"And you, Mademoiselle?"

"What did you say comes with the black bread?" Hedwig asked.

"Turnip soup."

"How is that served?"

"It is served in a bowl, Mademoiselle, at no extra charge."

"I will have that, please."

Herr Piehl disappeared into the kitchen briefly and returned with the women's meals and a bottle of wine. "The wine is from my private store," he explained. Herr Piehl settled into a chair and rubbed his hands together vigorously. "A luncheon with the ladies," he said wistfully. "How long has it been since we have done this?"

"I can hardly remember," said Hedwig. "But you understand why we can't come down more often, of course."

Herr Piehl waved his hands in the air and shook his head. "Of course, of course. Please do not think of me, dear Hedwig. You have to look after the family, both of you. I am only nostalgic for better times. Having you at my table again merely reminds me of how much we have lost."

Mother smiled affectionately at Herr Piehl and the women began their meal in silence, while their host looked on fondly. As were most government issued rations, the bread was a little stale, but the soup was hot, and Hedwig found if she dipped the bread into her bowl, it became tolerable.

"It's been a long time since I've eaten anything so warm," she remarked.

Although it was the middle of the day, the room was bathed in shadow. The light of the candle on the table gave the women an impression of intimacy while they ate.

In a moment, the swinging door to the kitchen opened a crack and Bosel's nose peeked through, soon followed by the rest of the dog. Bosel casually waddled over to the table, his toenails clicking on the hardwood floor as he approached. He sat next to my mother. She put her hand down for him to sniff, but instead, Bosel inclined his ear toward her hand and leaned into it. She rubbed the dog behind his ear and down his back.

"How are you, Bosel?" she asked. He closed his eyes, pressed himself against her hand and gave a long, deep sigh. "Oooh, does that feel good, Bosel?"

"Come, Bosel," said Piehl, and the dog obliged. Piehl broke off a generous portion of his bread and gave it to his pet. Bosel took the bread in his mouth, circled his mat, which Herr Piehl dragged inside for the winter. Bosel settled down in a pool of his own fur to eat. He licked it at first instead of devouring it all at once, Hedwig noticed, as if he knew there wasn't much left.

"What a dear," my mother commented.

Piehl sighed and rested his chin on his hand. "It's been hard for Bosel, too. They don't issue rations for pets, so I have had to scrounge for his food. I have nearly nothing left for him." He shook his head. "He's been very patient with me." Piehl crossed the room, sat on the floor next to his dog and hugged him. "He's such a good boy." Bosel looked up from his bread and licked his owner's cheek before returning to his bread.

"I have relied as much on him to survive the last several months as he has depended on me," Piehl continued, scratching Bosel behind his ear. "He has been an excellent companion."

"I understand how you feel," said Mother. "Since Wolfgang left, even though I have often been surrounded by people at the house, I am constantly aware that he is not there. If it weren't for the children, Herr Thienelt, and for dear friends like you and Hedwig, I don't know how I would manage."

"You should have a St. Bernard."

"Perhaps."

"How are your children?"

"As well as they can be on four hundred grams of bread a day. They are home right now. The Keitel girl, Helga, is playing with them today."

A smile almost flitted across Piehl's face, but his lips only tightened. He stood up, walked behind the bar and reached beneath it. He pulled out a cigar box and took his place at the table. "I have something for your children," he said. He opened the cigar box and sorted its contents: colored ration cards. "This is what I can spare," he said, pushing one of the piles to my mother. "They were Frau Hirsch's."

The women's shock at the sheer magnitude of their friend's unexpected generosity quickly faded when they realized what had happened. Frau Hirsch had died. Hedwig placed a chunk of bread beside her bowl and put her hands in her lap. The old woman's body, Hedwig realized, still lay upstairs, probably on the bed in which she died, still wrapped in the blankets Herr Piehl had given her. Undoubtedly, she would remain there, frozen solid, until the ground thawed or the war ended.

Mother touched Herr Piehl on the arm and squeezed it gently. "I'm sorry. You were very good to her. She had nobody." Herr Piehl began to gather his ration cards and placed them in the cigar box. "When did it happen?" she asked.

"Monday morning," he said softly. "She was breathing, but I could not wake her. I wasn't with her that night. She was so weak by then,

I could not help." He shook his head. "I am sure you will be able to make use of her cards."

My mother gathered the cards and counted them. Although they represented three weeks' worth of adult rations, they were still pitiful. "We still have some provisions," Mother said. "Would you mind if I gave them to the Keitels? They have three children who need these more." Herr Piehl shook his head. Mother tucked the cards into her purse and assured Herr Piehl the cards would not be wasted.

When the women had finished their meals, Piehl took the dishes into the back while Bosel, who had fallen asleep, puffed and twitched as he dreamed. When Piehl returned, Mother spoke. "Have you heard from your man Petersen?"

"Yes, I have," Piehl replied. "He went to Breslau on Tuesday with your Krugerrands and managed to trade them. He's back in town and says the Mark is worthless in the market. Next to bread, the most valuable commodity is alcohol. So I sent four gallons of vodka with him. Your fifty gold pieces and my vodka bought fifteen pounds of turnips, five blocks of gelatin, some bars of chocolate, linseed oil and five tins of toothpaste."

"Toothpaste?" asked Hedwig.

"If it's mixed with starch, it becomes something like pudding."

"When is he going to deliver it to you?"

"I expect it this evening," Piehl said. "I'll bring it by your place tomorrow morning. You understand I would rather not be out past dark carrying twenty pounds of black market rations."

"Thank you very much," Mother said. "And thank Petersen for me. We'll see you tomorrow, then." She rose and shook his hand. They said goodbye to Bosel and walked to the door.

The deadbolt clicked behind them, and they started back to the mansion. The icy wind picked up and hurled clouds of snow down the street. The old woman who had lost her bread cards was no longer there. Men with axes and saws stood in the street hacking chunks of frozen meat off of the dead horse's carcass. The dead man's boots had been stripped, exposing one torn stocking and a naked blue foot.

***

The next morning, Hedwig accompanied my mother to the Keitel house. The Keitels lived on a quiet street off of the main road in downtown Hummelstadt. On a summer day, the walk from our mansion to the Keitel house might take fifteen minutes, but their progress was hampered by the ice and snow.

They kicked their way sluggishly though the snow until they reached the low wooden fence lining the Keitel yard. One corner of the fence had been buried completely under drifting snow, and the gate was slightly ajar. The windows were dark and the house was silent as Mother and Hedwig approached the steps leading to the front door. Mother knocked loudly and waited for nearly a minute before knocking again. She noticed one of the front windows was broken and had not been repaired.

When nobody answered, Mother tried the doorknob, expecting it to be locked while the Keitel's were out, but the door opened. She turned to Hedwig. "Wait here. I'm going to see if anyone's in." She peeked her head inside and called out,

"Herr Keitel? Emma?" *Where is the dog?* she thought as she set her purse on a table by the door. The house was frigid.

"Helga, dear. Are you home?"

She entered the living room. Snow had blown in from the shattered window pane and had settled in a powdery stripe across the carpet and over Helga Keitel and her two older brothers. They had been laid beside one another with their hands folded across their chests and bloody towels wrapped around their heads. The German Shepherd, Tasso was on its side next to the oldest son. The mother, Emma, was lying unceremoniously against the baseboard of the far wall, crumpled and broken. She had been shot more than once. In one corner of the room, the wall was spattered with blood and brains. The pistol lay at the feet of Herr Keitel, who sat slumped in a wing-backed chair, from which he looked over the remains of his family. Below his neck, where the bullet entered, his clothes were saturated with blood.

Mother stood aghast, disbelieving the scene before her. "Frau Doctor?" Hedwig peeked into the room. "My God!" she gasped. Then she began to tremble and her voice rose to a panicked pitch. "What have they done? My God!" She ran into the kitchen, as if there might be something there that might explain or negate the horrific scene in the front room. She returned.

"I don't understand it! What happened?" Mother found a notepad on the coffee table. The top sheet was smeared with blood and writing in a desperate scrawl. She circled the table and read the note:

BY GOD I WILL NOT ALLOW MY SONS TO BE SCHUTZ-STAFFEL. I WILL NOT WAIT FOR THE RUSSIANS TO SLAUGHTER US ALL.

"Oh, Frau Doctor," Hedwig sobbed. "Helga played with the girls just yesterday! How could this happen? How can we tell the girls? Helga was their best friend!"

"I don't know," Mother said, biting her lip.

"We should at least cover the bodies, don't you think, Frau Doctor?"

My mother did not reply, but looked at the broken window, which she noticed was also splattered with blood. Hedwig went upstairs, stripped the beds of their sheets and covered the bodies. They were about to leave when Hedwig paused. "Should we take their ration cards?"

The grim logic pained my mother, but she agreed. "They'll go to waste if we don't." She then added, "But don't tell the children where the extra bread is coming from. They don't need to know what happened here."

They searched the drawers and shelves in the kitchen and pantry and the rest of the first floor without any luck.

"If the cards are on the bodies," said Hedwig, "I won't be able to take them." They went upstairs and into the master bedroom. While Hedwig picked through hatboxes in the closet, my mother searched the chest of drawers and under the bed. Under the bed, she found Emma's jewelry box. She opened it and said quietly: "I found them."

"What?"

"I have them. Would you count them, please?"

Hedwig took the cards and quickly added them up. "It seems like they are all here. A week's worth for the whole family."

"There was a little bread in the pantry," mother said with tears in her eyes. She felt like a vulture, but she knew what they were doing was only prudent. She would not let her children starve because she felt sentimental.

She retrieved her purse at the bottom of the stairs and followed Hedwig, averting her eyes when they passed the living room. They salvaged the bread, some sugar and a few turnips, the last scraps of food in the house. They left in silence.

***

That horrible winter passed and slowly the sun drew back the blanket of snow atop Hummelstadt. The trees and earth, indifferent to the suffering and fears of the citizens, budded and greened. The coming of spring, however, promised little to the town. It was clear the war in the East was lost and the Russians would take advantage of the weather and drive into Germany. We were terrified and devastated by what now seemed inevitable.

For years, the German media made the Russians out to be barbarous Bolshevik hordes of insatiable, bloodthirsty savages bent on enslaving Germany, leaving little to allay our fears. Our armies had driven into the Russian homeland, and if German reports were believable, they had disenfranchised a vast populace while inflicting heavy losses on the enemy. Nobody thought the bitter anger of the advancing Russians could be mollified in any way.

Hummelstadt was almost on top of the border with Poland and would be one of the first towns to suffer the wrath of the invading armies. We didn't know if the town would still exist come summer.

As Hummelstadt thawed, and as we shed our shabby bulks of winter clothing, mother decided Erica, Juergen and I had grown far too thin. Ration distribution had become increasingly unreliable to the point there were no longer goods enough to redeem ration cards. Pets and strays silently disappeared from the streets.

Finally, mother decided there was not enough food in town to keep her children healthy. The pervasive rumor was the nation's stores of food were decaying in the silos of rural farms. Prompted by these rumors, mother sent a letter to my father in Hildesheim, telling him to contact some of the wealthy farmers he had represented over the years and to ask them if they could host his children for a few weeks so we might build up our strength. A few days later, mother received a generous invitation from one of father's clients who owned a large farm near Glatz. We could stay with his family for a few weeks, provided we stayed out of trouble and helped with chores. Mother sent a grateful note to Herr Winkelmann, our host, saying we would arrive on the following Sunday.

Two days before we left, Erica and I accompanied mother into town on a frustrated trip to pick up rations. On the way back to the mansion, we stopped in at the Gasthaus zur Krone to see if Herr Piehl's black market contacts delivered anything she could buy.

The day was bright and warm, and I was excited to see Bosel. We found Herr Piehl inside the restaurant sitting by the window with Anne, the waitress, but I hardly recognized them. They had both lost a lot of weight. His neat appearance had given way to a disheveled and dirty look. His face was gaunt, his hair was tinged with streaks of gray, and his eyes were sunken and red. Anne also seemed much older.

The restaurant was otherwise empty and the tables and chairs had grown dusty from disuse. The only familiar elements were that his front door was unlocked and open to the fresh air. Herr Piehl did not stand to greet us when we entered, but smiled faintly and gestured for us to join them.

"How are you doing, Wally?" he asked. I noticed he had addressed mother by her first name.

"We've done better," my mother answered frankly. "We are coming back from the market, but didn't have any luck there. They told us to check back on Monday, but they didn't sound too optimistic."

Herr Piehl shook his head. "If you had come here first, I could have saved you the trouble——they were empty this morning. I don't know why they bother opening."

"Well, it smells like something is cooking," mother remarked. "Has Petersen been to the market?"

Herr Piehl's mouth drew tight. "He brought some bread yesterday. It's old, but still edible. The stew you smell is for Anne's family. They've had a very difficult winter."

"Did your sister have her baby?" mother asked Anne.

The waitress nodded. "About two months ago. It was a boy."

"How are they doing?"

"As well as possible, I guess, under the circumstances. The baby's healthy and nursing, but my sister doesn't get enough to eat. It's Sophie's first baby, and she's exhausted. My mother and I help her whenever we can so she can get some rest, but it's been hard. We're very grateful to Herr Piehl for the soup."

Herr Piehl smiled feebly, and sighed.

"You needed it."

"If you have any bread to spare, Herr Piehl," mother ventured, "I would be eager to buy it from you to get the children through the weekend."

"I have a little extra," he said. "I have two loaves you can have for what I paid for them." He got up slowly, shuffled into the kitchen and returned with the bread, which he had wrapped in newspaper.

Mother paid him with a gold coin and insisted that he take another.

"It's only fair," she explained.

"Soon, not even gold will be worth much," Herr Piehl sighed.

"Thank you."

With that, mother took her leave and led us home. I was disappointed we had not seen Bosel.

Erica and I left for the farm that weekend. Juergen was not interested in joining us. When we returned a few weeks later, Hedwig explained to us that Herr Piehl had slaughtered his beloved companion to feed Anne's family. Erica and I were both devastated, since we both considered Bosel to be one of our best friends. Sixty years later, I still get upset when I think about what happened to him. After Bosel died, I wondered how the war could get any worse.

On the Sunday we were to leave for the Winkelmann farm, Hedwig woke us up earlier than usual. We dressed in clothes she set out for us the night before, and we hurried downstairs, where our packed suitcases waited. We had old brown bread and water for breakfast. Erica was in a much better mood than I was. I felt a little tired from the early wakeup call. She was excited we were going to stay on a farm. We met mother at the kitchen table where she gave Otto a big envelope for Herr Winklemann. She was not coming with us.

When we finished our meager meal, mother sent Hedwig for Otto and the car. Before the war choked off the civilian supply of gas, Otto and my mother had the foresight to stockpile gasoline in the wine cellar. Mother had bartered most of it away in the last few months, but she kept enough to fill the Mercedes' tank three times in case an emergency arose. This was the first time we used any of it, and probably the only time we had been in a car since father left. Mother kissed us both and instructed us to behave ourselves. Otto would retrieve us in two weeks. She lingered at the door as we drove away. Juergen was not with us as he would be living at home on our combined rations while we were at the farm.

Even though I could hardly remember the last time I had been away from Hummelstadt, the scenery between home and Glatz did not interest me at all. Every kilometer or so, we passed an abandoned car at the side of the road. It was usually stripped bare. Otto, I think, drove as fast as he dared, either because he was under mother's orders to return as quickly as possible, or because he felt uncomfortably conspicuous as the only driver on the road. In hindsight, I suspect he was worried that we were a tempting target for strafing Allied planes.

At some point, I hunched over the suitcase on my lap and fell asleep, but awoke when the car began waddling down an unpaved, gravel road.

"We're almost there, I think," said Otto. "All this" he said, pointing to a field beside the road, "All this is part of Herr Winklemann's farm." From the look of it, Herr Winklemann was very prosperous. In fact, his farm was large enough, he had been able to avoid the draft.

After considerable jostling and swerving to avoid potholes, we pulled up in front of the Winkelmann house. While we dragged our suitcases from the car, a short, slight man, whom I recognized as a regular guest at mother's parties, emerged from the building. He had a square face and thick hair yanked across his forehead at an odd angle. Otto approached Herr Winklemann and introduced himself as mother's groundskeeper.

I had never known what Herr Winklemann did for a living, but he definitely failed to meet my expectations of a farmer. He was wearing work clothes, but was very clean for someone who spent all day in a field. His face was pale and thin. I had naively expected our host to be outgoing and friendly, like the farmers I read about in books. It was immediately clear that Herr Winklemann was not overjoyed by our arrival. He only allowed Otto to make the briefest introductions possible before sending him back to Hummelstadt.

"Come inside and get settled," Herr Winklemann suggested indifferently as he turned his back on the cloud of grit kicked up by the Mercedes. The exterior of the farmhouse was similar to ones I had seen near Hummelstadt. The first level was long and low, like a shoebox. The walls were stucco and had only a few small windows. The heavy wood door was in the middle of the façade. The top of the shingled roof was as high as the house was long, and it sloped sharply. Inside, the house was divided by a hallway that ran from the front door to the back wall. On the right, doors led into a barn and tool shed. The Winklemann's and their employees lived in the left wing of the house.

In the kitchen, Frau Winklemann, a fair-haired woman in a simple dress and apron, greeted us more cordially than her husband. Herr Winklemann then took us upstairs to the workers' quarters, where we would be sleeping. It was a long, sparse room furnished with rows of bunk beds, like a barracks. He left Erica and me alone to unpack. We stowed our clothes in the wooden chests near the beds. There were no windows, but we could hear the wind scraping a tree branch against the thin wall. Erica was not happy about having to share a bedroom with more than a dozen other people.

After a bit, Herr Winklemann came upstairs and told us we would be helping Frau Winklemann with housework. We followed Herr Winklemann down to the kitchen and he left Erica and me with his wife. She also showed us the water pump and the barn.

Frau Winklemann and an old woman, one of the worker's mothers, were washing the dishes from lunch. They had us drying the dishes and putting them away. The kitchen was at least as big as the one in our mansion, and an enormous wood table lined with benches dominated its center. Everyone on the farm ate breakfast, lunch, and dinner together, generating endless dirty dishes, and keeping the wood-burning stove cooking all day.

Once we finished with the dishes, it was time to start preparing dinner. Dinner was served cold: slices of meat, cheese, eggs and bread. There were also potatoes leftover from lunch. If there was nothing else to eat on the Winklemann farm, there were always potatoes. They were grown behind the house in a large produce garden that was kept by the workers' wives, and they were served with every meal. One of the kitchen tasks that Erica and I were responsible for every morning would be to gather potatoes that had been placed in the pantry and clean them for cooking.

At about six o'clock, the workers came in for dinner, and the enormous kitchen became cramped and noisy. Each worker had his or her own mug hanging by its handle on a peg on the wall. They each took it before sitting down at their assigned place on the benches. At this point, Frau Winklemann gave Erica and me our own identical stone mugs and told us that we were responsible for keeping them clean and never use anyone else's. She then took her seat beside her husband at the end of the table.

After that meal, Erica and I were satisfied. We were actually full, if not bursting, for the first time in several months. We had not even had overly generous amounts of food, but our stomachs were so unused to being full that they registered gluttony. Afterward, I felt warm and drowsy and wanted nothing more than to sleep. As soon as the meal ended, Erica and I had to clear the dishes for washing and dry them again.

At the end of the day, I had made a disturbing discovery. I asked Frau Winklemann where the bathroom was. I had casually searched the house when I had a minute, but could not find it. She led me outside to a wooden shed, and inside there was a bench with a hole in it. When she opened the door to show me the latch to lock it, a mouse standing on the lip of the hole jumped down and scurried through a gap in the wall of the outhouse. I stood not believing the only place to go to the bathroom was outside. But she closed the door behind me. I held my breath and went as quickly as possible. Later, when I told my sibling about the facilities, Erica said, "I saw it this afternoon."

"What if it rains?"

"It has a roof and walls. What else do you need?" I thought it was unsanitary. "There was a mouse in there when I used it."

"It was there when I was there, too."

I resigned myself to using the outhouse, but considered each trip an unpleasant excursion into country life.

By the time the kitchen chores were finished, most of the workers had gone upstairs to bed. Frau Winklemann told us she would wake us up the next morning.

Morning came sooner than I thought. Frau Winklemann did not have to come and fetch us, since the entire dorm seemed to rise automatically at 5:30. Once we had dressed and come downstairs, we had a breakfast of bread and lard and sausage before starting our chores.

After we had cleared and cleaned the dishes, Frau Winklemann sent me to help Frau Munsch, another worker's wife, to do the wash while Erica helped prepare stew for lunch. The wash consisted both of the family's clothing and linens and those of the workers (except for workers' bed sheets, which were not washed the entire time we were there). It was all done by hand on scrubbing boards with soap made on the farm. The laundry was a two-day job. On average, each worker had one or two extra sets of clothing, and each one was worn for several days. When Frau Munsch had finished wringing out a piece of laundry, I hung it out on the line to dry. I could never understand how such a small, fragile built woman could work so hard. She was very pleasant and happy to talk to me while we worked. Her husband had been disabled early in the war and returned to Silesia to work on the Winklemann farm. (Agriculture was a respectable, critical wartime industry). Frau Munsch had grown up in a small family and found she enjoyed the communal life on a farm. She said other children, relatives of the Winklemann's, had stayed on the farm all winter. I liked Frau Munsch very much.

Lunch was the biggest meal of the day. Erica and I couldn't believe how nice it was having so much to eat, after going hungry to bed nearly every night for so long. It was usually a hot stew poured over potatoes. Every three days or so we would also eat peas with thick hunks of bacon, and occasionally, we had apples. It was at lunch that Herr Winklemann fed his dogs--three large wolfhounds. After they gobbled their meal, they would slip under the table and put their big heads in your lap, waiting for scraps. We made sure they got every bite we spared. I knew if we were hungry, dogs would be hungry, too.

Our brief stay on the farm quickly settled into a routine. But one morning, Frau Winklemann told Erica and me to put on aprons, which seemed much too big for us. I remember Erica complaining about that. We filled them with corn kernels to feed her geese. We went down to a large pond which we passed as we arrived at the farm. The geese knew what we were there for, and a small armada of them crossed the water to meet us at the near shore. There were two pairs of geese, each with four or five goslings in tow. The two families were clearly rivals, and spent most of the time chasing each other away from the corn we tossed. The adults were aggressive and would peck at your closed fist if they thought there was corn in it. They would try to snatch the feed out of our aprons.

On this particular morning, the adults were extremely impatient, and I suddenly found myself surrounded by really large birds. I tried to back away carefully, but nonetheless was nipped in the arm by one of them. It didn't hurt, but it startled me and I thought the geese were attacking. I started to run, but did not drop the feed, so the birds kept after me as I hurried along the edge of the pond. As Erica tried to shoo them off of me, she scolded them like they were dogs: "No! Bad! No!" They made quite a racket, honking and pumping their wings as they chased me, seeming much larger than they actually were. After a few minutes of this, I started to drop feed, and they became distracted and were content to chase each other around the shore instead of me. After that, feeding the geese was a daily chore for my sister and me and the most fun part of our day.

The two weeks passed very quickly, but by the end, I had gotten a little homesick.

We did not return to school after Otto picked us up from Herr Winklemann's; the nuns had left. I can only imagine they were terrified by the stories of Stalin's persecution of religious groups, to say nothing of the Russians' hatred of Germans. Many of our friends had disappeared with their families, as had all representatives of Hitler's government. As a result, during those last days before the war ended, all commerce, social services, and transportation came to a halt in Hummelstadt and in other German towns. Nobody ever knew what had happen to Herr Piehl. The rumor was, that he might have left town or he might have starved to death.

The Breitkopf household spent the last days of the war at home. While we were gone, Herr Thienelt had closed the law office and encouraged Otto and the other employees, who had been reduced to a skeleton crew by this time, to return to their families. There was very little to do but brace ourselves for what was to come.

The only form of communication that remained was the radio. The station in Breslau continued to broadcast continuously as the Russians approached the Polish-German border near Hummelstadt, and what we heard about the advancing army was terrifying. Erica and I were horrified to hear that the Russians had not only taken Koenigsberg, but the zookeepers there had shot all of their animals. It was thought to be more humane than allowing them to fall into the Russians' hands. It was beyond the understanding of two little girls. Even Juergen was on the verge of tears.

On March 6th, I remember very well the Russians had crossed the border and were only a few kilometers away from Breslau. Two days later, very early in the morning, the Russians entered the city. We listened to the reports through the morning and into the afternoon, until the station stopped broadcasting. By then we knew, that in no time the Russians would be in Glatz, only by train from Hummelstadt. The announcer's voice was cut off in the middle of a sentence. Weeks later, we heard that Breslau was leveled.

The abrupt silence shocked me. It was as if someone grabbed me by the throat and cut off my air. The world suddenly became much smaller, and I felt a claustrophobic panic. Up until Breslau fell, we could keep track of how far away the Russians were. We could predict and plan, but now we didn't even have the illusion of control.

Mother was also clearly frightened by the silence. She raced out of the kitchen, and we heard her on the stairs. In a few minutes, she came downstairs with Hedwig and Herr Thienelt. Each was carrying a packed suitcase. "We're going to visit your father," mother announced curtly. She hurried us outside and into the Mercedes. Hedwig squeezed into the back with us while Herr Thienelt drove.

The road leading to the station became increasingly clogged with the abandoned cars of families long gone from Hummelstadt. They had been collecting there throughout the winter, but the town hadn't the resources to keep the streets clear. We pulled to the side of the road a few blocks away from the station and climbed out with our suitcases. We walked hurriedly to the entrance. Inside, the lobby was filled with families. I saw a lot of familiar faces, all of whom were waiting for a train west. Erica, Juergen, Hedwig and I joined them while Herr Thienelt and mother stood in the line at the ticket window. When they returned, Herr Thienelt had tickets in his hand.

"We couldn't get tickets out tonight," mother said, "so we got tickets for tomorrow evening. Everything else is sold out."

"We can try to board early and buy tickets on the train before then, though," Herr Thienelt added.

We settled in at the station to wait for the next train. We waited outside under the overhang on the platform so we could be the first onto the train when it pulled into the station. There weren't any seats in the waiting area, anyway. We sat along the wall for the rest of the afternoon and into the night with our luggage. By now, I had realized I didn't know when I would see home again. I started to cry.

"What's wrong, dear?" Hedwig asked.

"When are we coming home?"

"We'll be coming back after we've visited your father. I thought you would be happy to be going. You haven't seen him in a while. It's just a little vacation."

I calmed down after that, but by this time I was old enough to know better. The story about going to visit father gave me something to believe and a destination to reach. I was willing to let myself believe it.

Two trains passed through Hummelstadt that evening. Both times they stopped, nobody got off and the conductors who were standing in the doors said there was no more room. Through the glass of the coaches, we could see soldiers and civilians packed into the cars like cattle.

We were, of course, disappointed we could not board that evening, but we at least had tickets for a train the next day. After the day's last train departed, Hedwig asked if we should return in the morning.

"No," mother said. "We're not taking any chances. We're not going to lose our spot on the platform."

As the sun sank and night climbed into the sky, the temperature dropped on the platform where mother decided we would wait for morning. We got cold and fussy, so we went inside the station with Hedwig, while mother and Herr Thienelt huddled together outside. We sat on the floor and watched the traffic in the station thin, but only slightly. The attendants pulled the grates down over the ticket windows and locked their office.

We watched for a seat to open up so some of us might get some sleep. Eventually, a space opened up on a nearby bench against the wall, and Erica curled up on it with her head on a rolled towel and slept. I slept, albeit restlessly, sitting against the wall. I woke up every fifteen minutes or so to stretch my neck and try to get comfortable. Juergen was intent on staying up all night, but even he fell asleep, eventually.

When morning came, I was stiff and tired and my mouth tasted chalky and dry. It was about six o'clock when a fresh tide of citizens from the town started arriving at the station. They brought with them more cumbersome suitcases than those travelers who arrived the night before. They lined up at the ticket windows long before the windows were open. But the clerks, who had left the night before, did not return. We waited all morning with mother and Herr Thienelt, but none of the scheduled trains came-—none at all. Two hours after we were supposed to leave, it was clear we would not be leaving Hummelstadt by rail. Mother told us we were leaving, and we gathered up our luggage and walked out to the car.

"Aren't we going to see Daddy?" Erica asked.

"Not right now," mother said. "We'll try in a few days when the station is not so busy."

When we got back to the mansion, mother made us a small, unappetizing meal with the only food left in the house: raw eggs mixed with sugar. We were hungry enough to slurp down the noxious concoction, but we were still hungry. As night came, mother and Herr Thienelt sat in the kitchen and talked about what we would do next. They decided we could only wait for the Russians to invade and hope it would not be too bad, but there wasn't any minute we didn't think of it.

Chapter Four: Occupation

In the month and a half between the closing of the rail system and the arrival of the Russians, many people in Hummelstadt became desperate. A few relocated and left almost all of their belongings behind. Some of our friends disappeared from the convent school before it closed early in April. Others took up the local pharmacist on his offer of poison for anyone who would want it. (I did not know about this at the time, but such a course was remarkably common among those facing the inevitable occupation, and especially among people with close ties to the Nazis).

One day in April, Juergen took Erica and me to a field not far from the mansion. There we saw where a farmer had recently shot dozens of horses to prevent them from suffering neglect before he killed himself. Most of us, however, waited and hoped we would be able to stay in our homes once the Russians arrived. Juergen spent his free time in the kitchen, listening to the last broadcasts of German High Command on the radio. He was thirteen, my sister and I were almost ten.

Eventually the trains stopped coming through Hummelstadt. Food became even scarcer. Every morning, my sister and I came downstairs and asked if there was any food. We spent much of the day waiting for whatever food and Hedwig was able to find. One morning, after a breakfast of stale bread and water, Erica complained loudly to mother how little food we had and how hungry she still is. Most of the chickens we kept in the yard as pets had died from disease. Erica and I tearfully buried each of them. Only three remained alive.

As the day drew closer to Mittagessen, the main midday meal, there was an unusual amount of activity in the kitchen. A pleasant aroma emanated from a pot on the rarely stove. When we sat down at the long table to eat, Hedwig ladled out a hot chunky soap, the only hot Mittagessen I could remember in our house for a long time. It was delicious, but after a few bites, Erica suddenly grew pale. I looked at her surprisingly, but now she had covered her mouth with her hands. She got up and ran for the door to the garden without saying a word and vomited up everything on the steps. Hedwig followed and tried to comfort her.

At first, I didn't understand why she was so upset about the meal. After all, she had complained more loudly than anyone else about how hungry she was. I would have expected her to be happy, as the meal was much better than the horsemeat we sometimes ate. "Which one was it?" Erica demanded, but Hedwig and mother said nothing. When my sister ran outside, I realized what had happened. The meal turned to ashes in my mouth. I spit it back in the bowl and pushed it away. At mother's orders, Hedwig had kept us occupied upstairs while Otto had gone into the yard and slaughtered Dickus. I found it hard to believe I had been eating one of our pets. There was no way I could finish the meal. Mother must have felt sorry for us because she said nothing.

About this time, without our friend Helga, who mother had told us moved to Frankfurt, Erica and I began to play with the daughter of the butcher, Marianne Angelhorst. Marianne was a little bit older than us, about two years, and was already wearing makeup and taking an interest in boys. She was not a very bright student, apparently, because she had been held back a year and was in our classes. Mother did not like her much. She apparently agreed with father, who always said that one should surround oneself with intelligent people because maybe we'd learn something.

Marianne's parents were too old to have a daughter her age, naturally. Marianne was adopted. Frau Angelhorst was sickly. She had a heart problem that severely limited her movement. Nonetheless, mother occasionally hired the Frau Angelhorst to do some sewing when it needed to be done. Herr Angelhorst was pleasant enough and we were regular customers. They lived above their shop in the town square. Erica and I did not like to play at Marianne's apartment because one could always smell the butcher shop below.

Marianne's family was very religious, and this is one of the reasons we found her so interesting. She was rebellious and wore makeup, which we thought made her look glamorous. She was also destined to be quite a beauty, with dark curly hair, big brown eyes and long legs. My sister and I were almost ten and tall for our age, but we were very skinny and freckly. Marianne was always willing to give us beauty advice, which always involved makeup and irked our mother. Marianne would take my sister and me, identical, and give us different makeovers so we could see how makeup affected one's appearance. Of course, in these early days of experimentation, you could always tell Erica and I had been playing with Marianne because we came in looking like clowns who had been mugged.

Mother would occasionally let us have Marianne over for a sleep over. These "parties," as we called them, even though there were only three of us, were among the best memories I have during that time. We would go outside after dark and play hide and seek in the rose garden. The darkness added an extra degree of difficulty to the game. It was almost impossible to find the person you were looking for at night, and we jumped out and scared each other before running and shrieking back to the base.

On May 17, 1945, my sister and I planned to spend the afternoon with Juergen, who was taking us to pick wildflowers for mother. We would be going off of our property into some field that abutted our orchard. In April and May, Silesia is beautiful-—there were wide-open, unfarmed stretches of land blooming with Margaritten (white daisies) and Pfingstrosen (tiny yellow roses). But Juergen and Erica had moved too slowly for me that day. I waited most of the morning out in our orchard, hoping that seeing me might stir up some speed or pity or guilt in one of my siblings to come out and go flower-hunting with me.

At about 2:00 in the afternoon, Juergen finally came out onto the second floor balcony. I yelled at him to hurry up, that I was ready to go. He paid no attention to me, and after a minute or so, he called out pointing, "Monica! Tanks!" A low rumble I had not yet really noticed grew louder and soon echoed throughout the valley below our mansion and throughout the town. I ran inside and told Hedwig what Juergen had seen, and we both went upstairs to see what was happening.

By this time, mother and Herr Thienelt had joined Juergen on the balcony, and we all looked down into the town. The tanks were moving through quite rapidly; they crawled in on the main road from Breslau. There were no cannons or gunfire, just the sound of engines and the teeth of the tank treads chewing the main road. As suddenly as they arrived, the tanks and their rumble disappeared into the distance.

We were behind Russian lines. The war got real that day, and suddenly, the gracious, dignified life we remembered in Hummelstadt had changed. The quiet was tense. We didn't know what to expect, but we didn't think the invasion would be so silent or over so quickly. We did not even have time to put out white sheets to surrender. There had been no defense of the town, which we considered a mixed blessing; at least the Russians had not shelled Hummelstadt before invading. When the tanks were gone, they had left no Russians behind to keep the peace or maintain order.

Hedwig and Herr Thienelt found Erica and brought her down to the kitchen, where Juergen and I waited with mother. Mother's plan was to keep the whole family together and in plain sight until she was sure it was safe. For the next several months, like a mother lion and her cubs, my sister and I were rarely more than an arm's length from her.

A few hours later, Russian soldiers began to pour into Hummelstadt in trucks and on foot. Women came out and lined the street, offering flowers to the soldiers. These were not so much expressions of joy or liberation as they were a peace offering to solicit the good will of the Russians. The second the soldiers moved among these women, however, they began to grab and punch them. At first, the shots were sporadic, but they grew in frequency as the afternoon grew late and more Russians entered the town. Finally, mother ushered us upstairs to the fifth floor. She thought we would be safer there than on the ground floor, and we could see anyone who approached the house.

From the fifth floor, we had a good view of the Russian convoys passing through town. They sped and veered crazily as if the drivers were drunk, but they were likely just keeping pace with the tanks ahead.

Hundreds of truly drunken soldiers were making their presence known in the town, smashing shop windows and breaking down doors. The looting was spectacular in scope, and the damage the soldiers were doing was visible from the top of the mansion. Out of one window came a feather bed, which soldiers slashed apart and gutted so we saw white down litter the street. I doubt they found anything hidden there.

The most terrifying and foreboding aspect of the day, however, was not the Russians' disregard for property, but their treatment of the civilians. People were dragged out of their cellars and pushed out into the streets. They were stripped of their valuables at gunpoint as the Russians shouted, "Uhr! Uhr!" demanding their wristwatches. The soldiers then confiscated any food they found in the houses, leaving the citizens with nothing to eat.

Soon, another wave of Russians arrived but found no food or alcohol left to steal. They took out their anger on the civilians, shooting in broad daylight those with nothing left to surrender. Most bodies were initially left where they fell, and the Russians simply stepped around or over them. At least a dozen were dead and dying German civilians—men, women and children were piled alongside the road at the foot of our long driveway.

Had we lived in the center of town or if the Russians had arrived earlier, my family almost certainly would not have survived that first day. Our view of the Ring, the town square, revealed a surreal nightmare below that lasted for several days. The soldiers would demand, "Frau komm!"(lady come) and then the women were lined up and led off to the Provost's office. Later we learned that, once inside, the women were taken to separate rooms and raped continually for hours. It seemed well-organized and systematic, and any woman who ran or resisted at all was shot.

I remember very clearly an old woman, Frau Schmidt, who owned the bakery and used to give out treats to customers' children, stood on the roof of her store in her nightgown. I have no idea how or why she was there. Another woman, who worked for the grocer, was shot through the hip and lay in the street screaming in pain. Nobody came to help her and she died there. Frau Hoffman from the butcher's shop, we later heard, survived the first day by burying herself under slop in a pig trough. One woman, whose children we knew from the convent school, for some reason was leading her family (and their little dog) through the streets when she was confronted by a drunk soldier who screamed at her in Russian. She did not understand and, as punishment, was murdered in front of her children.

But through all the chaos and savagery of the first day, incredibly nobody approached our mansion. We all stayed inside (even though Juergen wanted to go into town and make sure his friends were alright). The only light in the house was a candle that Herr Thienelt had lit behind blackout curtains in the kitchen. That night, Erica, Juergen and I slept fully dressed in Hedwig's room. I did not sleep well and had a nightmare I couldn't remember. In the morning, I found myself in Hedwig's room and remembered what had happened the day before. I noticed my mother was not there and I asked, panicked, where she was. I was headachy.

"She and Juergen are downstairs in the kitchen waiting for you," Hedwig said.

Mother had not slept at all. After we had gone to bed, she and Herr Thienelt had gone downstairs to the kitchen to listen for any information on the radio, but there was little. The news they heard came in the sound of gunfire that lasted through the night. Sometime after midnight, someone had knocked softly on the kitchen door. When they answered the door, a Russian officer stood there and politely asked for a glass of water. The door was hastily locked behind him when he left. That was the only contact we had with the Russians during those first hours.

Erica, who had slept like a rock, came downstairs not long after mother told me this story. She was hungry and asked for food.

We did not dare leave the mansion on the second day. Herr Thienelt was clearly frightened, as was Juergen, who had assumed manly responsibilities for the family's wellbeing during father's absence.

This day too was full of strange sights. Those who had been shot or killed were still lying in a ditch of blood in the streets. That morning, a vast and smelly herd of what must have been thousands of cattle passed through the town. I later learned they were headed to Russia, and that farmers had to surrender all of their livestock to the Russians. They were only allowed to keep one cow for the time being. One sickly cow collapsed on the road, and it lay there suffering until it died.

After the cows had passed, I saw a German shepherd, a poodle, and a dachshund walking together down the road, following the column of cattle. The shepherd seemed to be the leader, and he kept looking back waiting for the poor dachshund, whose little legs could not keep up. I assumed they all belonged to the same family. The animals looked pitiful, and I asked mother if we could not take them in, or at least give them some water. Mother said absolutely not.

That afternoon, a column of uniformed German POWs under guard shuffled along the same road the cows had covered with dung. They looked very tired. Many of them wore bandages or limped or had eye patches or bruises. Like the cows, the POWs were also being prodded toward Russia, and had about the same chances of ever coming back. One of the soldiers was machine-gunned in the road. Possibly, he was tired and had fallen out of the column. Braver citizens lined the road offering cups of water to the boys.

The next morning, Hedwig noticed someone out in the garden wearing a German uniform. She went out and hurried the sick and terrified man into the kitchen. He was terrified, and Hedwig gave him some water. He told us he had been in the group of POWs we had seen the day before and escaped by jumping off of a bridge while nobody was looking. Juergen was very impressed by this. He knew if the Russians had caught him or saw him trying to escape, he would have been shot immediately. The soldier waited until dark and spent most of the day hiding under the bridge. That night, he had crept up toward the mansion to find some food.

The soldier's presence, of course, put the entire family in danger. If the Russians knew we had helped a German soldier escape, we would have been killed. We gave him a little food, and Hedwig suggested that he might have a better chance of fleeing to the west if he were dressed as a woman. She found him a dress, a jacket, glasses and a headscarf, and mother told him to dump his uniform far away from the mansion. He was very grateful and thanked us a dozen times before he slipped out the door. We never knew his name or what happened to him. Hedwig cried after he was gone as he reminded her of Paul.

In the months that followed, mother kept to the task of feeding her family. The ration system remained in place, but after the Russians arrived there was very little food left. Mother, therefore, took the risk of obtaining food on the black market, which was certainly punishable by death.

On the black market, one could buy meat (usually horsemeat) and other cheap foods, but not always. Often, mother returned from Herr Piehl's restaurant with nothing or maybe only a bag of flour. Farmers were accepting gold and jewelry for potatoes. I remember eating soup made of water and flour many times. Occasionally, our food was supplemented with an egg from one of the remaining chickens, but otherwise our options were few.

Following the arrival of the Russians, civilian movement was highly restricted. There was a curfew, and sentries were authorized to shoot anyone who broke it. Hedwig, for weeks, had been urging mother to let her go to Friedersdorf, a nearby town, where her family kept a farm. I don't think anyone I knew suffered more during the war than Hedwig's mother. She had lost both her son Hans and her husband to the war. The father's death was official, but the body was never retrieved. Hans had disappeared in battle in the East, and it was assumed he would never return. Such losses, however, were not uncommon when every family sent its able-bodied men to the Army.

Erica and I were together when Hedwig asked us if anyone wanted to visit her farm. We both wanted to go, but Hedwig said she could only take one of us. So, we tossed a coin and I won. I had been aching to leave the house for almost a month. I made this case to mother, and she surprisingly agreed that I should leave on the condition I stayed with and listened to Hedwig the entire time.

We left that night, before the sun went down and the curfew was in effect. Hedwig had made the trip a dozen times by bike over the last year, ever since her sister had fallen ill. I had accompanied her on a couple of trips. In the last months of the war, Margot's condition had worsened, and it had been nearly a month since we had been there to see her. On our last visit, Margot had been too weak to walk and I could no longer understand what she was saying. The doctor told Hedwig at that time that her sister's condition would eventually be fatal.

There was a road that connected Friedersdorf to Hummelstadt, but Hedwig thought the chances of running into a checkpoint or drunk soldiers was too great to take it. Before we reached the road, Hedwig and I ducked into some woods through which the road passed and took a path that was parallel to it. We moved as quickly as possible while there was still enough light to see, but once it got dark, we moved at a crawl. Hedwig held my hand tight as we wove as stealthily as possible through the trees. Every few steps, Hedwig stopped and listened, and hearing nothing, pulled me forward a few more steps. At times, we could hear engines or voices coming from the road. We assumed these were Russian voices and hid ourselves until the noises passed.

The trip was tense, and I felt at any moment someone would step out from the brush and surprise us. At one point, however, as we neared the outskirts of Friedersdorf, we heard someone behind us. Hedwig pulled me along a little faster and told me to keep walking. The footsteps picked up pace, and I could hear someone running clumsily through the woods behind us. I cringed and waited for the first gunshot, which never came. I almost screamed and ran back home when a man suddenly appeared out of the darkness and ordered, "Hedwig! Stop running!"

I could have cried. It was a German, a childhood neighbor of Hedwig's. I could not see him well, but he had recognized us as he had been heading in the other direction. In fact, he was on his way to fetch Hedwig when he saw us. He hugged her. "Your mother needs you at home, Hedwig. Follow me."

We followed the man back to Hedwig's home, and he left us at the family's doorstep, where Hedwig's calico kitty, Motte, greeted us. I was happy to see the friendly cat, who adored Hedwig and threaded herself between Hedwig's feet, purring. She picked the cat up, opened the door and let her inside.

"Mother?" Hedwig asked, knocking on the door. Soon, her mother came into the little parlor. Her face brightened and she hugged her. "Hedwig," she said, weeping, "Margot is gone."

I stood by, awkwardly, as Hedwig took in the news, disbelieving and stunned. She gasped and regained her composure. "When?" she managed.

"A few weeks ago, right after the Russians came."

It turned out the neighbor who guided us through the last stretch of woods had handled the burial arrangements under the noses of the local Russian garrison. They had been able to give Margot a proper burial.

But Hedwig's mother had been living in virtual isolation since her daughter had died. Mail was not gone through, and she had no idea whether or not Hedwig was still alive. She had become very depressed dwelling on the thought her entire family had been irretrievably lost to the war. She believed she and the cat were all that were left.

Hedwig remembered that day when her brother had joined the army. He was eighteen years old. It was voluntary at first to sign up if you wanted to be a soldier in the SS, as they needed soldiers badly. Nobody signed up.

It was a bittersweet reunion. I made myself as unobtrusive as possible, stroking the cat, which had fallen asleep in my lap as we sat in the kitchen. Hedwig cooked some eggs for me. I avoided eye contact with them as I ate, glancing around the small rustic house, its simple furnishings and tiny windows. The family had kept a lot of chickens and a large garden of carrots, lettuce, tomatoes and potatoes. Hedwig's mother had a rough go of it in the last couple of weeks. When the Russians came, they took the two healthiest cows and all the pigs. The last cow died shortly thereafter. After Hediwg and her mother talked for a while, we went to bed. I slept on a sofa in the parlor, exhausted from the long walk, while Hedwig slept in her childhood bed.

In the morning, Hedwig promised she would be back as often as possible. We stood outside the house under an immense oak tree as the women said goodbye. Hedwig gave her mother some gold she brought from the mansion, and we were on our way.

The route we had taken seemed to her to be safe enough to take now, as she could always make the trip on her bicycle during the day. Traveling in daylight, especially on a relatively isolated road, could still be just as risky as traveling after dark. The Russians didn't need an excuse to shoot you. Nonetheless, we arrived safely at the mansion before noon.

Despite the occupation, the town tried to go about its daily business as best it could. Keeping to routines was an important part of coping with the chaos around us. Herr Thienelt had closed the law business and sent the staff home to their families. He spent most of the day inside, attending to whatever chores he could find, venturing outside as seldom as possible.

The Catholic Church remained open throughout the summer, and we attended Sunday services sporadically. It was usually too dangerous to attempt to walk through the town. We prayed a lot at home, anyway.

The Russians had no respect for German privacy or property. We received orders to never lock a door, which was tantamount to inviting the Russians to wander in at any time of the day or night. Often, Hedwig, being alone in the kitchen, would be startled by a Russian digging through the pantry for food or alcohol to steal. (We found they had drained my father's wine cellar on the third or fourth day).

Given the very high likelihood of assault and rape in the town, women were forced to find ways of protecting themselves. The most common way was to dress as men, so as not to attract the attention of lecherous drunk Russians. Another way one could protect oneself was to befriend a Russian. Many girls started to be seen with Russian boys in uniform, and at night we could hear them carousing loudly in the town. Those families who didn't associate with the Russians looked at those women as traitors. It seemed like a political betrayal to the community. Many of the men they were out with were involved in the atrocities, but the fraternization pacified a number of them. It also extended a measure of temporary protection to the girls' families.

Meanwhile, the Red Army kept up a persistent hunt for Nazi officials. They followed every tip they received and dealt with the accused in a swift and brutal manner. As stated, a lot of the local Nazi leadership had fled long before the Russians arrived. They were scared to death. They had destroyed records and disappeared into the countryside.

The Russians, however, seemed adept at exposing people and accusing them of being Nazi. Almost anything could be interpreted as evidence of Nazi sympathies, including old travel papers, ration cards, hunting rifles and photos of family members in Wehrmacht (military) uniforms. If they weren't shot on the spot, the accused were taken to the

Provost's office, presumably for interrogation. Hedwig suspected most of the real Nazis ended up in such places, since they might actually have useful information, (even if they cooperated, I doubt any of them were ever released). But I suspect, oftentimes, accusing someone of being a Nazi sympathizer made it easier to justify the execution of an unarmed civilian.

Chapter Five: Our Polish Home

Despite the prominent location of our mansion, the property escaped most of the Red Army's looting. The only goods we had been stripped of had been the contents of father's wine cellar, some household supplies and foodstuffs. We weren't subjected to house occupying troops like so many other families in Hummelstadt. We had mostly been left alone. We kept to ourselves as much as possible, rarely venturing beyond the edge of our property.

This changed in early August, as the Russian troops were preparing to leave. Polish troops began to arrive in town to establish what would eventually be Polish civilian control.

One morning, an unannounced Polish soldier entered through our unlocked door and informed mother, in German, our mansion was to be the residence of the new Polish mayor, who would require the first two floors of the house. He gave mother fifteen minutes to make preparations. Mother dared not question the armed soldier. She and Hedwig quickly moved the suitcases upstairs they had packed in the first days of the occupation.

Mother assembled the household downstairs in a receiving line, much as she had greeted her party guests years before. She wanted to show the new mayor that our family was well mannered and courteous. We had no idea what to expect.

Mr. Kivisov arrived with an assistant, who carried the mayor's luggage and equipment. He introduced himself to mother in imperfect German and shook our hands as she, in turn, introduced us. He was a tall, imposing man of solid build and had a broad jaw. Deep creases like scars ran down his cheeks. He had dark wavy hair and a light mustache under a sharp nose. He was dressed in a striped suit and tie and clearly was of good breeding.

It was quite a jarring adjustment to have our lives confined to the upper floors of the mansion, and have these Poles overtake our house.

Kivisov initially had few fans among the family. As the acting male head of household, Juergen absolutely despised him. Erica did not like so many steps every time she went downstairs for a meal. Herr Thienelt, like Juergen, reacted somewhat like an animal whose territory had been encroached upon. This was especially obvious when it became clear that mother flirted with the mayor, who responded in kind. Strangely, I grew to like him very much. As the weeks wore on, Mr. Kivisov tried to make peace with his hosts by giving us packages of coffee and chocolate, which were nearly impossible to secure with ration cards.

My mother spent a good deal of her time with Kivisov, helping with his German, which was passable but not fluent. He seemed to genuinely appreciate mother's attention, and it turned out he was, like father, an attorney. With the exception of commandeering the first two floors, he behaved like a guest, otherwise, and made very little extra work for Hedwig. She became his attendant, of sorts. She would also make sure to save portions of the meals she prepared for him to give to the children.

He also made it possible for Hedwig to travel regularly to Friedersdorf by sending her on "official business." We made allowances for his presence and accepted his kindness—at least he was not a tyrant. While mother was, in principle, not pleased to share her home with an uninvited stranger, she maintained a sense of dignity by speaking to us about Kivisov as if he were a guest, whose privacy she respected.

Mr. Kivisov stayed with us for about three months. Then one day, without warning, he vanished. He came downstairs with his suitcase, thanked Hedwig, said good-bye and wished the family good luck. I was disappointed to hear that he had gone. I had gotten used to his presence and the preferential treatment he showed my sister and me. Even his staff did not seem to know where he was going.

Later, we heard rumors he had been arrested by Polish police, perhaps, I thought, for being too kind to Germans. Some said he had fled to Italy. Others heard he had been given a diplomatic position in London. Of course, the only proof we had was his absence. He left the house the way it had been before he went away; it was as if he never existed.

A few days later, Kivisov's replacement arrived, and we were all disappointed. We greeted him in the same way we had Kivisov, but that was the only similarity between their two stays. His name was Chevolek, and he was a bloated little man with a pockmarked face and a red nose that looked ready to burst. He was a sloppy, grotesque authoritarian and barely paid us any heed as he entered the house. He had an air of a dictator, and it was immediately clear he had taken an immediate disliking to us or a total disinterest.

His companion was a tall, slim, vivacious woman named Sasha who looked to us like a movie star. Her first act as First Lady was to commandeer the third floor for herself. Mother again had to move all of our possessions up one more flight. She was dressed as if she was going to a party and wore heavy makeup all of the time. She was Chevolek's girlfriend, and she ordered Herr Thienelt and Juergen to bring in her suitcases, as if they were common workers. I was stunned she could possibly have so many things—-including dozens of hatboxes and lots of clothes. I resigned myself to the possibility they might stay with us for a very long time, a long time, indeed.

Physically, Sasha and Chevolek were an unlikely pair. She was shapely and elegant with dramatic, stunning features. He was a troll. What they lacked in physicality, we soon learned they made up for in temperament. They both drank hard, entertained themselves almost constantly and were indifferent to the upkeep of their residence-—our residence. At times during their tenure, the mansion resembled a fraternity house. People breezed in and out at all hours and they held riotous parties almost every night. Their friends and associates dirtied the floors faster than Hedwig could clean up. Sasha took Hedwig to be a sort of personal servant, and called on her at all hours. She ran poor Hedwig ragged.

These parties were the most enduring image of Chevolek's tenure at the mansion. They were nothing like the parties mother used to throw, and I irrationally felt in some way they threw them to spite her. At mother's parties, we heard singing and light laughter and music. At Chevolek's parties, we heard shouting, women squealing, arguing, and occasionally, fighting. Chevolek's guests brought their own alcohol and often showed up drunk. When the weather was pleasant, they spilled out into the garden, where men could wander off to urinate in the fountain, vomit in the rosebushes, or fornicate with their dates in the orchard.

Such lewd and outrageous behavior was torture to my mother. At one such party, she went downstairs and asked that the revelers please keep quiet; it was after 3:00 in the morning. Chevolek slapped her in the mouth. Mother disgracefully came upstairs crying, as the guests laughed. Mother never crossed him again. She knew he could do a lot worse to her.

Under Chevolek, the situation in town grew increasingly worse, and the abuse of women by our occupiers became more prevalent and open. Chevolek had taken a complete disinterest in the welfare of the town. Women were routinely taken by force to the police station, and if they returned, they had been raped and severely beaten. More often, the women were simply raped in their homes. More than one husband had been forced to watch soldiers gang-rape their wives and then was shot for protesting.

Once the charity we had received from Kivisov was withdrawn, my family again started to feel hunger pangs more frequently. Juergen was so disgusted by this, he decided he was going to do something about it.

One morning, about a week after Chevolek arrived, Juergen left the house without mother's permission and hurried down to the marketplace. The streets were mostly empty and he made it down to the grocery store without any trouble. He intended to break into the grocery and rummage about for whatever food remained. When he arrived, however, a sentry armed with an automatic weapon was guarding the entrance. The soldier spied him and said the dreaded words, "Komme her." (come here) Juergen froze. The soldier, who was not much older than my brother, approached him and looked him over. He asked Juergen a question, presumably in German, but my brother could not understand him. Juergen instead put his hands up.

The soldier laughed, patting his back, and motioned to Juergen to put his hands down. Then, against all expectation, the soldier stepped back and opened the door to the grocery store for Juergen, who stood there in disbelief. The soldier winked, and Juergen realized he was not about to be shot in the street. Juergen moved slowly to the grocery store and started to look around. The shelves were bare, but behind the counter he found a small package of sugar. He looked up, and the Polish soldier was looking the other way, as if he were keeping watch for Juergen.

My brother approached the soldier and showed him the package of sugar, just to make sure there had not been a misunderstanding. The soldier nodded and said in a low voice, "Go home quickly." Juergen ran off with his prize.

My mother's reaction to this was mixed. She was grateful the soldier had not shot Juergen, of course. She made my brother promise not to do anything like that ever again. The soldier's behavior was a rare instance of compassion in an otherwise hostile world. I'd thank him today if I knew who he was. We hid the package from Chevolek and ate the sugar sprinkled over bread, which was often our only food, anyway.

The next morning, two armed soldiers barged into the mansion and demanded to see the owner of the house. The children spent a lot of time in the only common area on the first floor: the kitchen. Since the weather had grown chilly, the wood burning stove kept the room warm at all times. All three of us were together in the kitchen and none of us moved a hair. Hedwig called upstairs to mother, who was on the third floor. She came downstairs and the soldiers told her to put on a coat.

My heart leaped into my throat. Where were they going? Where were they taking my mother? I felt as if I was in a dream, detached from myself and seeing all this without understanding, as Hedwig handed a coat to mother. And then mother left.

"Where are they taking mother?" Erica asked Hedwig.

Hedwig had the same dazed look in her eyes as the rest of us. "I don't know," she said." Wait here." She ran upstairs to find Herr Thienelt.

We went to the window and watched as the soldiers marched mother into town at gunpoint. Herr Thienelt joined us. "Come with me, children," he said, and he took us upstairs to Juergen's room on the fourth floor.

The upper rooms were more sparsely decorated, since they had not been intended for full-time living. Hedwig was waiting for us, and Herr Thienelt told us to wait while he talked to Chevolek. But Chevolek was not yet awake, still recovering from the previous night's rowdy party. We had to wait upstairs for him to rise. (For some reason we felt safer there).

Chevolek finally came to in the early afternoon. I was not there for Herr Thienelt's conversation with him, but when he returned, he said, "That bastard is worthless," the only time I heard him swear. Chevolek did not know why she had been arrested, nor did he seem to care. "All he knew was she was probably arrested and probably taken to the police station. The soldiers are probably looking for Nazis."

"Can't he help?" Hedwig asked.

"If he wanted to, he probably could," Herr Thienelt conceded, "but certainly he didn't offer."

"Did you ask?"

"Of course." He said he was not going to interfere in the Army's business. He then addressed us directly, "Your mother has been arrested, and I don't know why. Until she gets back, you have to be good."

For the next few days we felt like orphans. In late May, we heard from the Red Cross that father had become a British POW, and shortly after that we had gotten a letter from him saying he was not harmed and expected to be released soon.

As the war reached Wilhelmshaven, he had been issued a gun and sent in to fight. His slapdash unit surrendered to the first soldiers they encountered. Soon thereafter, we received another letter saying he was going to be freed, but because he could not travel in Soviet occupied territory, he intended to move to Hildesheim. But we did not hear from him regularly—weeks, sometimes months passed between letters. And now, mother was gone. I was devastated not knowing where our future was headed next. Tears filled my eyes.

Hedwig was really the one who tried to comfort us, but the trembling and fear remained because we really had no idea of what might have happened to mother.

We kept busy, or rather, we were kept busy by Sasha, who seized the opportunity to assume authority over the children. We spent a lot of the next few days cleaning floors and walls with Hedwig, trying to scrape off the accumulated filth of Sasha's parties. Aside from our new chores, she paid the children no attention. I don't think we would have been able to make it without Hedwig, who assumed all motherly authority over us.

Deep down, I knew my mother was dead. About two days later, Herr Thienelt told us he had heard from mother. He told us she was visiting a friend in Bad Dekova. It was an irrational, misguided, and insulting attempt to make us feel better, and I did not believe a word of it. I had heard too many stories about women who had been arrested and never returned.

One of the women who disappeared had been a teacher at my school, Ms. Gerlach. I could not allow myself to hope for anything better for my mother.

After five days, mother returned home on foot. Erica called out to me that mother was coming up the walk, and we ran out to meet her. I could not believe what I saw. It was bitterly cold and she did not have her coat on. Her face was swollen and covered with bruises. Her lip had been split. She was beaten almost beyond recognition and suffering from what would become pneumonia. She didn't say anything, but Hedwig took her inside and helped her up the stairs. Chevolek was inside the door, but merely looked offended by her appearance.

Only much later did we learn what had happened during those five days. Mother had been taken to the police station, where she was led to an office and questioned. It was clear from the questions they were trying to establish that my parents were Nazis, which she vigorously denied. They seemed to assume that my father must have had some political affiliation with the Nazis to enjoy such a spacious house. This was, in a sense, true. No German under the Nazis could be expected to own a business if they were not somehow affiliated with the Nazis. This did not mean they had to attend political meetings, however, or even explicitly endorse Hitler's regime. The Nazis founded various special-interest clubs across the country that satisfied the requirements of membership. My father, who was profoundly apathetic about politics, had joined a motorcycle club that was run by Nazis, as he had no other choice but to act very diplomatically. We didn't know how much father hated to attend those meetings. Father had never even owned a motorcycle; he had to rent or borrow one when he attended club meetings. Such low level involvement in the Nazi party was necessary to maintain one's professional standing and allowed him to continue to practice law. I doubt, however, my mother even admitted to that, since, in her captors' eyes, it would have been enough to convict her.

After the interrogation, my mother was thrown into a cell with a young woman who had been beaten and raped. The cell window was open to the cold air outside, and the woman was very sick. Mother was soon taken to another room and raped for hours by several men before she was returned to the cell. The woman was gone, but she soon was carried back and deposited on the cold floor. Mother was beside herself and terrified.

The woman had presumably been raped again. She died in front of my mother shortly thereafter. Mother was taken again into the room and again raped repeatedly.

When she came home, she was dazed and had no idea of how long she had been gone. Time to her had not been measured in days, but in terms of how many times she had been raped. She lost count. She was convinced she was going to be raped to death, since they clearly had no interest in keeping her alive. They did not feed her the entire time she was there. She had occasionally been given water.

Hedwig cloistered my mother in her room and sent Herr Thienelt to Bad Dekova to find Dr. Heartel. Mother was bleeding badly and was very weak. In the meantime, Hedwig washed mother and did what she could to make her more comfortable.

Dr. Heartel was a general practitioner and one of the most popular and conspicuous people in Hummelstadt. He was known for his generosity, nobility, and prodigious height. While his office was in Bad Dekova, about one hour away by foot, many of his patients lived in Hummelstadt. He was accustomed to making house calls. At the end of his day, he often stopped for a drink at Herr Piehl's restaurant, where he always knew someone and he always picked up the tab.

I had met Dr. Heartel at mother's parties. He was a talented singer and often sang while my father played the piano. He was typical, I thought, of the type of people with whom my parents associated before the war. He was accomplished, intelligent, well-educated and wealthy. He lived in a spacious apartment above his office, which did a brisk business. His clientele in Bad Dekova were generally far wealthier than those in Hummelstadt. He kept every appointment, regardless of whether or not the patient would be able to meet his fees. He was one of the few local people who could converse with the Russians in their own language, and this helped keep his practice and estate largely intact immediately following the invasion. He was often impressed into service as an interpreter and a mediator, when needed.

His first wife had died while he was in medical school, but he had remarried. He met his second wife, Hilde, through a newspaper advertisement, which was not uncommon in Europe back then. Frau Heartel was a refined woman who shared her husband's cheery disposition, and they each had their own Mercedes'. The doctor shared my mother's passion for travel, and he and his wife took two or three long trips every year. Mother never traveled with them, but when they returned, she often invited them over to talk about their trip.

Dr. Heartel arrived a few hours later. Hedwig carried his things upstairs and guided him upstairs to where mother lay. Herr Thienelt, his cheeks red from exertion, stripped off his coat and paced the fourth floor in a helpless rage. He had worn himself out trying to keep his emotions at bay, and the full emotional impact of the last few days had caught up with him all at once. He and mother had grown very close over the difficult months, and the thought of those soldiers violating her visibly hurt him.

When Dr. Heartel emerged from my mother's room, he explained the situation to Hedwig and Herr Thienelt. She had been badly beaten, which was obvious, and bruised over much of her body (which Hedwig had already seen). She had a concussion and some of her back teeth had been knocked out. She was dehydrated and had suffered from exposure. She had clearly been raped. She was cut inside the mouth rather badly. Her lungs were raspy and he said she had pneumonia. She was young and would probably heal. He was satisfied the bleeding had stopped, but was concerned about how her lungs sounded and her concussion. He was also concerned about her mental wellbeing, since she had been through such a horrible experience.

Dr. Heartel offered to stay for a few days, since "Wally" was such a longtime friend. He thanked Hedwig for her help and returned to mother's side. We would be able to see her when she was feeling better. Therefore, we did not see her for a couple of days; she did not want us to see her so beaten and swollen. Only the adults saw her. Nonetheless, Erica and I sent in drawings of flowers via Hedwig and little notes that we loved her and we were glad to have her back.

Her pneumonia had cleared by the time we were allowed to see her. She cried when she saw us. I was thankful to be near her again, but in some ways it was an awful reunion. Mother was vulnerable in a way we were uncomfortable with. The bruises were still vivid, and they instantly dissolved any childish belief in my mother's (and my own) immortality. It was frightening.

Mother kept to bed for two or three weeks. We stayed with her often, but she spent a lot of time crying. Every humiliation had been forced onto her. She was shattered. The slightest noise startled her and was understandably a victim to sudden, intense, uncontrollable sobbing. Physically, however, she was healing and regaining her strength.

Dr. Heartel attended to Mother for about three days, until he was satisfied she would succumb to neither pneumonia nor concussion. He hugged us goodbye and said to call on him whenever he could be of service. It would be about three weeks before mother was strong and steady enough to venture back into everyday life. Though she mixed among the Poles, she had much the same suspicion as a feral cat.

A few days after my mother's convalescence ended, I was awakened in the middle of the night by screaming. At first I thought it came from another of Sasha's decadent parties. But I quickly recognized my mother's voice. My first thought was that the police had returned for her. I jumped up and ran downstairs. The stairwell between the first and second floors, however, was blocked by two of Chevolek's subordinates, who were struggling with a large rolled rug. I followed behind them, not understanding.

At the bottom of the stairs, mother was yelling at Chevolek. He raised a fist and stepped toward her; she shrank back covering her face, sobbing. Herr Thienelt yelled in protective indignation from the landing, "Don't you dare lift a hand to her!" If there was ever a point at which Herr Thienelt was going to redeem himself for his inability to protect mother, this would have been the moment. I doubt that Chevolek even understood what Herr Thienelt said. He glared at Thienelt and made it clear, in German, to an armed soldier (who I had never seen before) that if we interfered in any way, to shoot us all.

Mother instinctively grabbed me and guided me upstairs, dragging Thienelt with her. From the window, we could clearly see what was happening below. One by one, mother's antiques, artwork and valuables were being loaded into a truck: Oriental rugs, a couch, paintings, silverware, clocks. Chevolek was relieving us of anything of value, including the Vermeer—a rare, priceless treasure that Chevolek could not possibly appreciate.

"It's not important," Hedwig reassured us. "We're all okay."

In the morning, mother could not bear to go downstairs. She waited in her room as Hedwig took an inventory of the family possessions.

Chevolek had done a good job selecting what to put in the truck. The rooms seemed larger and now were filled with echoes. The wood floors were exposed and cold. They had also been dinged and gauged by the soldiers' rough handling of the heavy furniture. I could clearly see where our grand piano had been dragged across the floor leaving chipped and chewed edges on the doorframe through which it had passed. I never heard Chevolek or Sasha play the piano. My siblings and I stood in disbelief in what was suddenly an unfamiliar place.

"Why?" Juergen wondered out loud.

When mother came downstairs, she showed no feelings. Her look was sullen and horrified. The man who had sat at our table for weeks had ransacked the first three floors, the whole time intending to leave us with nothing of value. It was another violation and betrayal that mother could not deal with emotionally.

At least he took Sasha with him. What a relief especially for Hedwig, as she had to be her butler day and night.

***

Now that Chevolek was gone, we figured the mansion was truly ours again. There was nothing left to steal. For the next few days we attempted to reclaim our house, cleaning the stink of Chevolek out of the floors and walls. But soon again, we were visited by an officer who told us we would be hosting another mayor. This time, he would have his entire family with him, as well as a sizeable, full-time domestic staff. We had four days to clear the fourth floor; we were going to be consigned to the fifth.

The fifth floor was already prepared for temporary living. Long ago, mother placed beds up there for visitors and for those too tired to drive home after one of her parties. Again, we moved our suitcases up one floor. Mother grumbled that before long we would be sleeping on the roof. Nonetheless, she thought a family might be an improvement over the drunken orgies of Chevolek.

The new mayor's name was Goblinsky. He brought his wife, his daughter and son, a staff of about ten, a strange-looking old dog, and a cat named Susie. Any play space we had gained when Chevolek left instantly evaporated. The new family lived on the first three floors and the staff on the fourth. The dog limited its movements to the family's floors, and the cat had the run of the entire house.

Goblinsky was a tall, slim man with glasses and a good command of German. His dark hair had receded, but he was nonetheless handsome in his own unusual way. His wife was short, heavyset and plain. His daughter, whose name I don't know, looked like her mother and did not seem to be interested in the mansion. She was a sixteen year-old ghost; she tended to lurk indoors with a book. She rarely went out and I only occasionally saw her in the kitchen, the communal space on the first floor. She was plain and uninteresting. I was interested in the arrival of the animals far more than that of the family. The dog was arthritic and did not move around much. I almost never saw it because it kept mostly to the second and third floors.

We Breitkopf children developed a special affection for the Goblinsky's cat, called Susie. She was pure white and as sweet as any cat I have ever known. Susie even charmed mother, who had never allowed us to have an indoor pet. The closest we ever came to pets were the utterly unaffectionate chickens in the yard.

It distressed mother and Hedwig to no end that the Goblinsky dog was often spotted curled up on a chair. But to have an animal like Susie in the house that responded vocally to our attention was especially gratifying. She almost never stopped purring. She freely moved between floors and could occasionally be spotted out in the yard. Mostly, she slept by the wood burning stove in the kitchen.

The only human member of the Goblinsky family with whom my siblings and I had any regular contact, was the son, Juris, who would be the pest of the house. He was perhaps a year older than Juergen, but was wild and clearly mentally defective. He was a cruel and sadistic bully. His parents, however, seemed to not notice what a monster they spawned and did nothing to correct his behavior. As far as I could tell, he considered all of Hummelstadt to be his personal property, and the Goblinsky's never dissuaded him of this notion. He acted on whims and never seemed to reflect on the consequences of his actions.

What confused me about Juris's behavior was that despite his complete disregard for civility, he was not a complete idiot. The boy knew enough German to get into arguments with my sister and me. I was perplexed at the time, but now I suspect he was simply a sociopath. He was fascinated with torture and death. His special fascination was Hitler, and he would endlessly pester an uncomprehending Juergen about Hitler and the spectacular violence he had inflicted on so many people. Juergen was not comfortable with this subject, but he tried to keep the weird little kid happy. To a large degree, that was the primary service the Breitkopf children provided to the Goblinsky's.

During the occupation, Christmas came curiously early to my siblings and me. This was because father was not going to be home that year. We knew it would be impossible for him to get permission to travel across country, and even if he could, we wouldn't want him to come into occupied territory. Ironically, the safest member of our family at that time was the one who had been drafted into the military.

Months before Christmas, about the time that Kivisov left, mother gave Erica and I what we thought was a strange task: writing Christmas cards and letters to father. Immediately after the war, the mail system in the East was medieval. I am also certain that all of our communications were monitored. Even though we had written to father regularly during the war, it did not seem to make much sense to continue at the same pace when it took seven to eight weeks for our letters to make it to West Germany. When letters arrived, they arrived in batches--a single delivery might include letters from three different months.

Mother sat us at the kitchen table and told us to write some Christmas cards for father. I remember I drew a picture of a Christmas tree decorated with candles. About the only benefit of having Goblinsky living in your house was that mail could be sent without leaving the house. We simply slipped our cards into the stack to be picked up downstairs near the door.

In a way, I was afraid of this Christmas. It had always been my favorite holiday-—even better than our joint birthday or Easter or Thanksgiving. But, I knew we would be lucky to even have a Christmas. The previous year had been rather bleak.

A few days before Christmas, a stack of letters from father arrived. Each child received three very long letters. The timing was so perfect that I considered them to be the best Christmas present I could get. Unfortunately, father's handwriting was nearly indecipherable, and as mother read them out loud to us, she tried to fill in the blanks as best she could from context.

The custom in Germany was to put up the Christmas tree on Christmas Eve. During that part of the celebration, mother would always send the children upstairs for a "nap" so she could prepare. Because we used real burning candles to decorate it, we made sure our tree was always fresh.

Otto was still on my mother's staff, but there was much less for him to do in the winter. He mostly cleared walkways and handled rare repairs to the building itself. As was generally the rule, he came on an as-needed basis during the winter. Mother asked him to get a small tree for us. He found one in the woods at the outskirts of town. It was so small, he had no trouble carrying it home in one hand and setting it up on the kitchen table.

We waited anxiously on the fifth floor for Hedwig to ring the gong, which signaled us it was okay to come downstairs. Unfortunately, the loud clang carried the real risk of irritating the Goblinsky's, so Hedwig rang it a little earlier than usual so as not to wake anybody. When we heard it, we leaped from our beds, changed into our clothes, and all rushed downstairs as fast as we could. Customarily, the first kid down got to open the first present. We weren't wearing our Christmas best, like we usually would. There were no new outfits this year, and our clothes smelled like hand soap because of a cleaning powder shortage. And even though there was a good chance we would not get anything at all, we still ran downstairs since it was the tradition.

I was delighted to see the cheery little tree lit up with candles and was surprised by a little stack of presents around its base. We settled down around the table and had dinner. Normally our Christmas dinner would include goose dumplings and all sorts of meats and wines. This year, it was a simple meal of potatoes and horsemeat. I did not distinguish between horsemeat and beef, but Juergen did. He declined to eat it. In the years before the war, we would receive dozens of presents each, but because we had received so little due to the war years, the few packages we found beneath the tree seemed as grand as any other Christmas we had ever had.

After dinner, we opened presents. Hedwig had somehow found the time to knit some red gloves for my sister and me. Juergen got a book from Herr Thienelt. (By this point, it had been at least nine months since we were last in school). Herr Thienelt was also able to give my mother something, and mother gave Hedwig a ring, which Hedwig treasured.

After the exchange of presents, we helped Hedwig clean the dishes and blew out the candles on the tree. We then filed into the music room, where it was our custom to sing "Silent Night." Normally, we would sing while father played on the piano. Singing without the piano only highlighted how far away we were from father this Christmas and that we had no idea how long it would be before we saw him again. I saw my mother was crying.

One morning in January, Juergen was in the garden and saw smoke curling up from behind the shed. He went to investigate and found that Juris had built a small bonfire back there. The boy was crouching beside it with Susie in his hands. Juergen watched in horror as Juris causally tossed the cat onto the fire. It shrieked and leaped off of the pyre with its fur smoldering with the deranged little boy in pursuit. Juergen had never seen such inhumanity. He grabbed Juris and asked him what he was doing. The boy said, "Putting the cat in the fire."

"Why?"

"I don't know. Just to see."

Juergen was dumbfounded. He explained that he should never be mean to an animal, especially a pet. "If a cat loses its whiskers," Juergen explained, "it can't smell anything." This, of course, was not true, but Juergen still believed it. The boy said fine, that he would just play with the cat.

Of course, Juergen could not tattle on Juris to his parents; they would probably have accused him of it. The little scene ended. Juergen went inside to tell mother what happened.

Later in the afternoon, Juergen was concerned about Susie and resolved to keep her away from Juris as much as possible. He went into the yard to look for her. Juris was long gone and the fire was out. Beside the shed Juergen saw the cat lying flat on her side. He ran over to her and scooped her up, but she was dead. Her neck was broken. Juergen screamed in frustration and fumed. He set her down and stomped upstairs to tell mother what he had found. She went out to see the remains and asked Juergen if he would bury the cat in the orchard, which he did.

Erica and I could not comprehend what had been done to the cat. So many pets had died during the last year that one more ought not to have shaken us. The other animals, by in large, had been slaughtered for food by desperate, heartbroken owners. This death, however, was simply senseless, cruel entertainment.

Juergen took the death of the cat as a personal insult, especially since he had tried to save the cat and was ignored. We already feared Juris, since more than once, he had bloodied Juergen's nose for a variety of imagined offenses, this son of a mayor was very strange.

One of his favorite petty insults was to stand in the stairwell and prohibit anyone in my family from coming downstairs, saying his father had told him to. This was, of course, a lie, but there was little we could do. After the incident with the cat, however, Juergen's patience had worn thin and his dignity would not endure another insult.

We soon had a heavy snow, and Juergen, Erica and I pulled our sleds from the shed. We intended to share them with Juris, who would inevitably join us in the yard when he heard us. Our driveway ran atop a little rise that was good for sledding. We had our fun for a little while before Juris came out. He unceremoniously yanked Juergen's sled from him and slid down the hill. Juergen had pure hate in his eyes as the boy raced down the hill on his sled.

When Juris had walked up the hill for another run, Juergen said, "Give me the sled. It's my turn." Juris simply turned his back on my brother. Then, without further warning, Juergen took a cheap shot, shoving Juris down onto the ground from behind. Juris hit the ground hard, totally surprised the meek kid he'd pushed around for months dared touch him. Juergen then jumped on Juris, turned him over, and beat the crap out of him. Erica and I stood in awe of our brother, realizing the seriousness of this event. We ran inside to find a German adult.

Mother had been watching from one of the windows and grabbed a coat. We ran into the kitchen and told Hedwig to come with us, but by the time we got to the door, mother was already outside prying Juergen off of the dazed, bleeding boy. Juergen was screaming incoherently at the bloody boy, who was covering his face. As mother pulled Juergen off of Juris, Juergen planted his boot squarely in Juris's crotch. Juris howled in pain and doubled over in the snow. Herr Thienelt brushed past us to help, and bent over the blubbering, vanquished bully. Mother spoke hastily to Herr Thienelt, and dragging Juergen, started down the driveway toward the road.

By this time, Goblinsky came out and shouted at mother to bring Juergen back, but they only quickened their pace. Goblinsky, who was not dressed, swore violently in Polish and then in German. He said to Hedwig, "Dem werden wir es aber geben."(Just wait and see what we will do to him). I half expected Goblinsky to fetch a gun and take shots at them right then. He didn't. He would wait for them to return and then demand his revenge.

Mother told Herr Thienelt out in the yard she was going to take Juergen to Dr. Heartel's apartment in Bad Dekova. Hedwig knew Erica and I would want to know where Juergen and mother were. We recently came so close to losing mother, we were terrified without her. That night, Hedwig told us what had happened, but warned us not to tell anyone where they were.

Actually, nobody ever asked me where they were. Goblinsky seemed happy to have mother out of the house, and began to take liberties, opening it to parties, of which Chevolek would have been proud. The adults drank constantly and were unpredictable. Erica and I kept to our room on the fifth floor for the most part. This kept up for two weeks, until one morning, mother and Juergen returned. None of the Poles seemed to notice their arrival.

It turned out that something big was going on in Bad Dekova that made it impossible for mother and Juergen to stay with Dr. Heartel. When soldiers arrived at Dr. Heartel's apartment and ordered they had ten minutes to pack their bags and vacate the building, Dr. Heartel urged mother and Juergen to slip out the back and go home. They stuck to the shadows and woods as they sneaked out of town, but behind them they could hear screaming and crying. Whatever was happening, they were thankful to get away.

***

The Goblinsky's threw numerous parties. They began after dinner, and Hedwig was recruited to act as a server during the affairs. Mother feared the Goblinsky's would be as horrid and rowdy as Chevolek, but this was not the case. In fact, while the parties could still be heard on the fifth floor, the Goblinsky's maintained order during their uproar. Their guests, like Chevolek's, were local Polish officials and army officers, but this crowd seemed content to sit around and talk and occasionally, late at night, sing. Nonetheless, Hedwig was stunned by how much schnapps and vodka these Poles could consume without dying. She wondered how they managed to walk home at the end of the night.

While Juergen was gone, one morning, I went downstairs. I was approaching the stairs down to the second floor, when Juris appeared in front of me. I had the feeling he had been waiting for me. His face was bruised and his lip was puffy. I tried to ignore him, but he would not let me past. I didn't say a word to him, and tried to let him know with my disinterested look that he had been taken down a peg in my book since Juergen had beaten him up. He didn't seem to notice my disdain, however, and said, "would you schlitten ?" Something about a sled was all I understood, and I shook my head. He stepped right up into my face and growled something in a mixture of Polish and German. Intimidated once more, I asked him to repeat the question in German and stepped back. He charged and punched me in the nose.

I hit the stairs but managed to scurry past him down the steps. I could feel blood running down my face and back into my throat. He did not follow me. I reached the kitchen, where Hedwig was looking out the window. When I saw her, I burst into tears. "Oh, Monica," she said, pulling a folded white towel from a stack on the counter. "What happened?" I was beside myself and could hardly choke out a word between sobs and lightheadedness. I had bled through the towel pretty quickly, and Hedwig got me another one. She told me to lay my head back to stop the bleeding. She stepped outside and brought in a packed handful of snow, wrapped it in a towel and put it against my face. In a few minutes, the worst of the bleeding stopped, but I would have a black eye.

I stayed inside all day. I had lost my desire to play in the snow. Juris had humiliated me absolutely, knocking me over with a single punch. Hedwig told me whenever I saw Juris to just go into the nearest bathroom so he wouldn't follow. (We still were not allowed to lock our rooms).

A short time later, Erica came downstairs. She was furious, almost to the point of tears. Juris had gone into Juergen's room on the fifth floor and stolen the electric train set that Juergen and father had played with together before the war. Then Juris had gone through the room and destroyed as much as he could. Later, once Juris had gone outside, I went upstairs to see what he had done. The damage was pretty extensive: he hurled a lamp across the room, upended and sliced open

Juergen's mattress, broken a window, torn pages out of several of Juergen's books, popped Juergen's soccer ball and pulled everything—all of Juergen's toys and decorations off of all the shelves. The trains were missing.

When Hedwig saw this, she called Juris the most hateful, evil boy she had ever seen. We set about cleaning the room and repairing what we could for when Juergen returned. As we worked, I wished Juris every painful death I could imagine. Hedwig continuously reminded us to keep our mouths shut.

As we sat in the kitchen, Otto entered and pulled Hedwig just inside the pantry to speak with her out of earshot of the children. Mother had told him to go and slaughter another chicken in the henhouse. Hedwig was not afraid of slaughtering a chicken and she saw them primarily as food, not as pets. She, after all, had been raised on a farm where chickens were slaughtered regularly. But each time mother had a chicken slaughtered, the children took it so hard they could not eat it. "Listen," she told Otto, "tell Frau Breitkopf I will have something for everyone tonight."

That night, the Goblinsky's were having an unusually large party. Hedwig had banished the children to the upper floors so she could prepare the meal. Throughout the occupation, Hedwig had been able to sneak small portions of food out of the mayors' meals to give to the children. On this evening, a prodigious amount of food was going to be prepared, and Hedwig would be able to take quite a lot without anyone noticing. There was no need to slaughter the chicken, at least not tonight.

In the evening, as the Goblinsky's and their guests ate, Hedwig sneaked two large trays of food upstairs to the family. We feasted on the Goblinsky's spiced pork, sausages, bread and fruit (which we had not seen for a long time). After our meal, I was full and drowsy and relaxed, maybe for the first time in weeks. If Hedwig was able to pull off little heists like that whenever the Goblinsky's had a large party, life might be occasionally bearable.

Hedwig, however, responsible for our feast, was not able to share it with us. She had to attend to the party downstairs. She assured us she would be able to eat leftovers.

Chapter Six: Exile

The next morning was February 17th, 1946. Hedwig was preparing the main meal for the Goblinsky's. It was almost 11:00 and my family was gathered in the warm kitchen. Here, literally in minutes, my life would change forever. I witnessed a bizarre scene that I would never forget.

A woman, whom I had never seen before, entered the kitchen from my father's office. Her clothes were unremarkable, except they were shabby, made of coarse material. They caused me inadvertently to think she was some sort of peasant. She brought with her two sickly and hollow-eyed children, presumably hers, whose attire was similarly ragged. They looked like Ignorance and Want in the Dickens' novel. They were all covered with snow and their faces were red. Reaching into her purse, she walked directly up to mother. She pulled something out and pressed it into mother's hands. "Hide these" was all she said before dragging her children out the kitchen door. We watched them slip into our orchard and vanish into the snowy woods.

The strange woman had deposited a gold ring and about two-dozen loose diamonds and rubies into mother's hands. We were all stunned. After a moment, mother realized how dangerous it was to be found with such riches. Mother, like so many other Germans, buried most of the gold Krugerrands before the Russians arrived. Mother had Juergen bury them in the orchard, but I have been told that most Germans hid such valuables in graveyards, where their ancestors guarded them.

I have since wondered what this woman's story was. Had she stolen the jewelry and was trying to hide the evidence? Whoever was found with stolen property was likely to be shot, and she certainly did not look like the jewels could be hers. But then again, perhaps that was part of her original plan. She might have been a wealthy widow from one of the nearby resort towns working her way east disguised as a common person, someone nobody would suspect of carrying such valuables. Maybe she had been discovered. I will never know. We never saw her again.

Mother, on the other hand, had suddenly inherited the strange woman's troubles, whatever they were. She suspected the jewels were stolen and asked Hedwig for one of the potatoes cooking on the stove. Mother quickly stuffed the jewels into the potato and told Hedwig to throw it out.

A few heartbeats later, five Polish soldiers with machine guns stormed into the kitchen and addressed mother in the most basic German: "Raus in dreissig Minuten." (Out in thirty minutes). And they left, apparently to serve other evictions.

It was as if someone had slid a knife into my gut. I couldn't breathe and I started to tremble all over. Hedwig started crying. I was simply unprepared for this; I had never considered we might be evicted from our own house. It was my last naïve thought. I'm sure now that my mother, Herr Thienelt, and Hedwig knew this would probably happen.

Mother told the children to come up to the fifth floor with her. We needed to get our suitcases, she said. We followed. She grabbed our coats and handed them to us. When she reached the second floor, she started to cry. As we climbed the stairs, I noticed that the Goblinsky's were nowhere to be found. They clearly did not want to be present during the eviction, lest there be an unpleasant or awkward scene.

We followed mother to her room, and she closed the door behind us. She dove into the closet and pulled out three suitcases: three small ones and two large ones. They were already packed. Mother returned to the closet and picked up a pile of dirty clothes at the bottom. Beneath it was a pile of jewelry, watches, and precious stones. She had hidden them there in case this day came (and to protect it from unwanted guests).

Mother divided smaller pieces of jewelry and stones into small portions and gave one to each of us. Then she produced a new outfit for each of us. "Change." Hide these in your clothes," she said. She showed us what she meant, placing a few of the jewels in a warm hat and pressing it tightly onto Erica's head and pressing it down tightly. Mother took none of the precious stones, but filled her coat pockets with Krugerrands, large pieces of costume jewelry and a few watches. She hoped if we were searched, they (Polish officials) would assume this woman had naively placed all of her precious items in her pockets.

The children's pockets remained empty. Into our new clothes, she had sewn hidden pockets in which to hide the jewelry, even in the underwear. The children all changed right there and began to fill the secret hiding spaces with the jewelry. When they were filled, the clothes were uncomfortable and lumpy, but the jewelry was hidden.

Herr Thienelt came to the door. "They're downstairs," he said solemnly. "Let's go."

We made our way downstairs. My mind had not yet caught up with what was happening. I had allowed everything to happen around me since they had announced we were to leave, and all I could do was respond mechanically to direct orders. There was really no time to think--nor was there a need to. Mother had taken care of that.

We filed downstairs to the kitchen, where the soldiers were smoking, laughing and leaning on the counters. "Open your suitcases," one said. One by one, Hedwig, mother, Herr Thienelt, Juergen, Erica and I set the suitcases on the table. There was little to take from the suitcases, only some fancy pens that Herr Thienelt had brought with him when he originally moved in. They opened mother's suitcase and removed the contents, but it was filled with dusty black paper photo albums with string bindings, some letters, a few important identification papers for the family and only a few clothes. One soldier examined each item of clothing, while another felt inside the lining of the suitcase, which yielded nothing.

"Turn out your coat pockets," one said, and we did. Mother's costume jewelry and watches spilled out onto the floor, and the soldiers eyed them, divvying them up among themselves.

Once they had confiscated everything mother had on her, the soldiers began searching each family member. A soldier patted Juergen down and then told him to come with him into the law office. We waited nervously for a few minutes. I expected to hear a shot, but none came. Juergen came out and looked apologetically at mother. Then it was my turn. In the law office the soldier patted down my clothes and told me to strip, which I did, trembling and ashamed. As he turned my clothes inside out, I saw a pile of jewelry piled on a desk, undoubtedly what the soldier had taken off of Juergen. He found everything I had hidden on me and told me to get dressed.

When I came out, Goblinsky had returned and was speaking in Polish to one of the soldiers. He turned to Hedwig, "You will stay here" and walked back to the mansion. Like the jewels, apparently, Hedwig was too precious to take with us.

Hedwig stood beside us until the guards had finished searching us. Then one of them pointed to the door. As we left, each of us hugged Hedwig and said goodbye. I could not stop crying. I was so scared for her. Leaving her behind plagued my conscience for years. We were devastated and speechless.

We stepped out into the garden with our suitcases. That was all we had and the clothing we were wearing. I felt so sad. The snow was coming down heavily, but I could barely see it through my tears. I was terrified, and I couldn't believe what this war had done to us. I was crying too hard and the frigid wind was stinging my eyes. Everyone was crying. We followed Herr Thienelt through the garden and past the henhouse, where our chickens remained. "Can't we take the chickens?" my sister said between sobs, but nobody could answer. We all knew they had to stay. Another wave of hopelessness hit me as I realized we were leaving them behind, too. Maybe Hedwig will take care of them, I thought. It was as close to hope as anything I allowed myself that afternoon.

The huge iron gate was frozen shut and Herr Thienelt had to force it open. I wiped my eyes and turned back to look at the only home I had ever known, the only place I could think of as ever calling home. I felt like a boat that had come loose from its mooring and was carried out to sea. I tried to look back at the mansion one more time. I saw the house outlined through the veil of falling snow. Our castle was real. We were leaving the five story mansion we were born in. Erica put her arm around me, and we held each other up as we trudged along the snowy path, uncertain of where it ended.

Chapter Seven: Displaced Persons

We had literally been turned out into the snow. It was bitterly cold. We trudged up the lane, which dipped and led up a hill. It was narrow, not much wider than a biking trail, and it was rough and uneven. Even worse, it was icy, and lugging our suitcases up the hill without falling was difficult. Mother was regaining her composure and started to plan how she could get her family through the next twenty-four hours. The frigid day promised a wickedly bitter night, and we were not dressed to sleep outside. We certainly would have frozen.

Mother decided to get us out of the cold as soon as possible. Once we reached the top of the hill, the path leveled off and led to a row of two-story apartment buildings. About four buildings down lived a mathematics teacher from the convent school that my sister and I had attended.

During the last year in school in Hummelstadt, we had Frau Kammer for math. Because Erica and I had difficulty with the material, my parents got to know her socially. Erica and I were good students. We found courses like history and social studies to be very easy, and I was especially good at languages. Since we were in the same grade, we were perpetual study mates. Between the two of us, we were always able to work our way through even the most difficult homework. It turned out, however, that neither one of us had an aptitude for math. This is not to say we were ever at any risk of failing her class. Erica and I were actually good students. Our father demanded it. Father assumed we were as intelligent as he was, and we worked hard to prove that to him. He expected our grades to be perfect-—and they were, except for math.

Mother had invited Frau Kammer over to the house a number of times to discuss our progress and to arrange for extra at-home math exercises. I only mention this because I have found that in America teachers and parents rarely have such personal social relationships.

When we arrived at Frau Kammer's door, she had no idea that we were coming. I can only imagine her shock when she opened the door to five people with suitcases. "Frau Doktor Breitkopf?" she asked. "What happened? Why are you crying?"

Mother explained our situation, and Frau Kammer said without hesitation, "Come inside," holding the door open for us.

She told us to take off our coats and make ourselves comfortable. Frau Kammer was in her mid-fifties, and kept her graying hair tightly tied in the back of her head. She dressed in very conservative clothing and looked rather masculine. She might have been intimidating to little kids if we did not already know her and love her as a teacher. Her two-bedroom apartment occupied the entire first floor, and she had a spacious parlor lined with shelves of books.

She ushered the children into her kitchen and soon produced three cups of hot chocolate-—an unheard of extravagance and unexpected treat. She told us that it had been her favorite since she was very little and she always managed to have a little on hand, even during war rationing. It was soothing and warmed me quickly, and for a moment I almost forgot what had just happened to us. As we drank our hot chocolate, Frau Kammer offered to share her house with my mother for as long as we needed shelter. Mother thanked her, sobbing. When she gathered her composure, mother insisted we would make more permanent arrangements as soon as possible.

That night, we had a satisfying meal of potatoes and cottage cheese. After the meal, the adults sat in the parlor and talked quietly. The parlor was too small for all of us to sit comfortably. Frau Kammer gave the children some books to read. I could hardly concentrate. Images from that morning kept me perpetually on the verge of tears. The low-talking of the adults in the next room was interrupted occasionally by a gasp or my mother's crying. After a while, Frau Kammer showed us where we could sleep. Frau Kammer would sleep in her regular bedroom, of course. Erica and I would sleep together in the guest bedroom on a narrow mattress, and mother would sleep on the short couch in our room. Herr Thienelt would sleep on the couch in the parlor, and Juergen would bed down in a nest of sheets on the parlor floor. We were packed in one on top of the other, but we were thankful we had somewhere safe to sleep that first horrible night.

In the morning, mother gave Herr Thienelt a list of some of father's clients who might be able to help us. Mother wanted to move out of Hummelstadt, if possible, because she did not want to see the mansion. It conjured up too many memories just then, and we did not want to remind ourselves of our eviction if we could avoid it. When I heard mother explain all this to him, the reality that I probably would never see Hedwig or the mansion again took hold of me.

Herr Thienelt spent the next few days hunting for a new place for us to live. Father's connections had been able to help us in the past, but we had never asked for so much in such uncertain times before.

In the meantime, my siblings and I passed time with Frau Kammer, who kept us occupied by giving us books. For most of the week, I turned the pages, but didn't really read. I could not concentrate. My life at that point was reduced to waiting for the next meal and remembering our home. Actually, despite the fact we were unexpected guests at the home of a single woman who was presumably living on limited rations, we ate pretty well at Frau Kammer's apartment. Mostly, I think it was the novelty of having something other than potatoes and horsemeat that made the cuisine memorable. Our lunches were still a thin soup made of flour and water, but I was awe struck by the ever-present hot chocolate and cottage cheese. We were okay and content and so thankful for Frau Kammer.

After a few days of unsuccessful searching, Herr Thienelt finally found a place for us to stay. It was with the Zimmer family, who lived outside of Bad Dekova. My father had helped Herr Zimmer, a childhood friend, set up his business, which sold sports equipment and pool toys to rich tourists before the war. Once the war began, however, tourism petered out to nothing in the spa city of Bad Dekova.

At the end of the week, we prepared to leave Frau Kammer. We would leave at night, after the curfew. At this time, Germans were generally confined to their hometowns and did not enjoy freedom of movement. A displaced family carrying suitcases would have attracted attention, and if we were outside of Hummelstadt's town limit, we would have been shot. Before we left, Frau Kammer let each of us take a book from her collection of children's stories. I picked a thick illustrated edition of fairy tales and put it into my bag. We hugged her one at a time as we left, and set out into the night.

It was a little after 10:00 p.m. when we headed out into the woods behind Frau Kammer's building. We could not take the roads. Mother had warned us about how dangerous our walk to Bad Dekova was going to be and she told us to be as quiet as possible. Erica and I would hold hands and walk in the middle, she said. Juergen would hold hands behind us, and Herr Thienelt would lead. We stepped behind a snow-covered bush at the back of the small yard that Frau Kammer shared with her upstairs neighbors and slipped into the woods.

Normally, a trip on foot to Bad Dekova might take a half an hour by the main roads. Juergen had walked that route by himself once to see a movie with a friend. Because we were taking back roads, cutting through the woods, and trying to carry suitcases stealthily, it would take us about and hour and a half to reach safety.

The crunch of the snow under our boots sounded thunderous as we tried to keep quiet. We crept carefully through the bushes and brush until we came to the Wanderweg that connected Hummelstadt and Bad Dekova. "Wanderweg" literally means "wander way." These are unpaved but well-worn hiking trails popular among Germans. They are usually well-marked and maintained and often scenic.

Before the war, my parents often took lunch guests down to one of any number of local trails to wander for an hour or more. It was a social outing, and proper casual attire was necessary.

On this particular trail, there was a bench and a trash can every ten minutes or so. Mother chose this path because she knew it well. It was far from any streets, and it almost directly connected Frau Kammer's apartment and the Zimmers' building. Even in the dark, we could see it had been used recently. The snow had been trampled into ice in a number of places. On our right was an open field. On the left were the woods. I was concerned that someone would spot us a long way off from the field or soldiers might ambush, rob, and kill us from the brush. Both were real possibilities.

We kept a steady, hurried pace. Erica had a hard time keeping quiet, asking the one question asked ever since cavemen started taking their children on migrations: "How much farther?" Mother initially hushed her, but after a while, when the pestering became insistent, she told me to walk holding Juergen's hand. She would walk with Erica to keep her quiet, presumably by squeezing Erica's wrist.

The Zimmer family lived on the fourth floor of an apartment building outside of Bad Dekova. Mother thought it would be safe for us to try and get there at night, since we would not have to cross any large roads or pass through the center of town. It was almost midnight when we arrived. We did not have to knock. Herr Zimmer was waiting for us.

His family received us warmly. They lived in an attractive modern apartment building. It was brightly colored and rows of balconies stretched all the way around the upper floors. In the foyer, mother hugged Herr Zimmer and thanked him profusely for his generosity. She was crying again, which made me feel uncomfortable. I knew if mother was comfortable enough crying in front of them, they could be trusted.

We took off our snowy shoes and coats and entered the apartment to meet the family. The two children were in bed. Mother apologized for tracking snow up the steps, since the custom at the time was that apartment tenants were responsible for cleaning the entire hallway leading to their door. The higher you lived, the more steps you had to clean. Frau Zimmer reassured her that it was not trouble and that she was happy that we had made it safely.

The apartment was larger than Frau Kammer's and was well appointed. It had handsome hardwood floors in the common areas and carpeting in the bedrooms. The architect of the building, however, seemed to have a fascination with light green. The exterior of the building and the hallways, as well as the tiles in the kitchen, bathroom, and balcony, were entirely light yellowish-green.

What I remember most about that night was that I was, for the first time in a week, able to take a proper bath. I remember being surprised by the fact there was no shower. The Zimmer's bathed in a large freestanding bathtub that was large enough for me and several of my friends. It was certainly a waste of water, but I filled it and soaked in the warm water for a long time. I would have been happy to sleep there if my mother hadn't knocked on the door and told me to get ready for bed. Again, Erica and I shared a bed in one of the two extra rooms. This time, however, Juergen slept on the floor next to us while mother slept in the other bedroom. Herr Thienelt had to make do with another couch.

In the morning, we ate eggs and bread. I felt invigorated by the good night's sleep the night's walk had made possible. We met the Zimmer's children (whom I did not remember ever meeting). The boy was our age, while his sister was about sixteen and did a lot of the housework. She was too old to take much of an interest in us small girls, but she was a gracious hostess and sweet.

During our stay with the Zimmer's, Mother forbade us to leave the apartment complex. She did not want anyone to know we were from out of town without permission. Anything could happen to us. So we kept busy in the apartment building.

Mother made sure we earned our keep. Every other day or so, Erica and I helped Frau Zimmer clean the stairs. We helped with meals, which I enjoyed, and helped the daughter with the chores. We had begun to settle into a comforting routine. I found I was happier the less I thought of Hummelstadt and our house, so I kept as busy as possible. Although, at times, unwelcome thoughts and sickening waves of nostalgia and loss still overcame me. We also wrote letters to father, telling him where we were and what had happened at the mansion, reassuring him that we were fine. We would be there soon.

One strange occurrence sticks out when I think back on our times at the Zimmers' apartment. They had a maid who came every day to the apartment to clean. She was a Polish lady, and she was hardly able to speak any German. The day after we arrived, Mother had unpacked my clothes and spread them out across the bed I shared with my sister. This little old cleaning lady, whose name I don't remember, came in to do the floors. As I sat there with mother, we witnessed this sixty-year old woman pick up a bundle of my clothes and put them in her purse! I couldn't believe it. Right there, with the owners looking on, this sweet granny was trying to steal my clothes! Mother seized the woman's bag, took out my clothes, and told the woman to get out. I couldn't believe that anybody, especially a little old lady, could be so callous and steal from people who had just lost everything they owned.

Still, nothing we had been through could ever prepare us for more horrible war news. By now, we all found out as the secret unraveled, and I believe the whole world knew, Hitler murdered nearly six million Jewish people in the concentration camps like Auschwitz, Bergen-Belsen, Nauen, Dachau, Dora, and others.

In the Buchenwald camp, the infamous Dr. Joseph Mengele, conducted torture experiments on twins. Many prison guards at the concentration camps were from Hitler Youth. Thousands of people were starved and tortured until they finally died. The townspeople of Weimar were led on a tour by American Military Police to see the truth in Buchenwald. Speechless and stunned, they saw the naked bones and bodies of hundreds of Jewish people.

To the German people, it seemed the world had come to an end when this terrible news unfolded and was out in the open for the first time. Because nobody was able to listen to foreign broadcasts, it was kept secret for many years. People just couldn't believe it. Mother was devastated and wondered why, not knowing anything like mass murder was going on outside our area. She looked dazed and horrified while, once again, tears came streaming down her face.

For the first time, I understood that Hitler was a murderer! A family by name of Hentschel, friends of my parents and a client of my father, lived on a small farm a few kilometers from Dachau. They told us years later, how often they noticed smoke in the sky. They had no idea where it came from. They found out what Hilter was doing much later. Of course, they couldn't believe it. By the time they knew the truth, the whole world was in mourning.

Chapter Eight: Life in the West

One morning, about a week after we had lived with the Zimmer family, I heard heavy boots stomping on the stairway, a rapping on doors, and men shouting in the halls. I looked out the window and saw the flashing lights of Polish police cars idling in the car park. Erica woke up when I got out of bed (she had not been sleeping well since we were evicted), and mother came in and told us to get dressed. As we did, a knock came on the Zimmers' door. It opened and two armed soldiers came in. Herr Zimmer came out in a robe, but before he could ask what was happening, the soldiers told him he had ten minutes to vacate the apartment and was to bring no luggage. They left.

Mother stood aghast, but Herr Thienelt said to me and my siblings, "Put on as many of your clothes as possible. It's very cold out." Erica and I were able to get on most of what I had in our suitcases. We both looked ridiculous and bloated when we finished.

The soldiers returned and told us we were leaving in two groups. My family and Herr Thienelt would be in the first group. Frau Zimmer hugged mother goodbye, just in case we were not sent to the same place. We never saw them again.

We joined about fifty other tenants who were standing outside of the building under the guard of armed Polish policemen. In a few minutes, we were told to report to the train station. We followed the crowd as it started to shuffle off for the station. Everyone in my family was holding hands so we would not be separated.

The walk to the station was short, about fifteen minutes. It was an exceptional cold day for this time of the year, and a very cold breeze was blowing in my face. I never felt that cold before.

My first impression of the train station was how tiny it was compared to the crowd that gathered inside and around it. The inside waiting area of the station was no bigger than the kitchen of our mansion. There was no way we would be able to make it inside, and the soldiers directed us around the building out onto the platform. At the end of the platform, we were instructed to show identification papers, which mother provided.

The platform was covered but the wind whipped freely and fiercely through the station when we arrived. There were only a few other people on the platform early on, so we were able to find an open bench. New groups of Bad Dekovans were arriving every few minutes, however, and before too long, the platform was teeming with thousands of shivering civilians. The entire town was being forcibly ejected from Silesia. We did not know our final destination, however, and rumors circulated throughout the crowd.

When the Russians had pulled out of town and been replaced by the Poles, my mother knew the Poles were going to annex our part of Silesia. We had little knowledge about what would happen to us once that took place. The rumor we feared most was that we would be shipped off to Siberia.

As the hours wore on, a few people started succumbing to the cold, mostly very small children. Every so often a wail would rise up from the crowd as someone discovered their baby was dead.

At the entrance to the station, a woman pleaded for room to come in so that she could change her baby. It was too cold out on the platform and there was no place to change her. That baby froze to death in her wet diaper.

The crowd was divided by the police into two groups, but many families were broken up by what seemed to be an arbitrary sorting process. Luckily, ours remained intact. One man tried to cross the platform to join his wife and children, but he was shot dead as he hurried across the divide. As far as I could tell, many children who had wandered too far from their families were essentially orphaned right there. It was heartbreaking to watch parents trolling through their assigned group asking if anyone had seen their lost children. To see crying children call out for their parents was painful.

One little boy with a runny nose asked me if I knew where his mother was. He was maybe four, but I could not get his last name before he wandered off. I burst into tears and prayed he'd find someone who knew him.

As the day was starting to break, we heard an approaching train. When it arrived, the train was so long I could not see the last car. It was not designed for people, but was a train for shipping cattle. As the Polish guards unlocked the doors, mother again told us to hold hands so we would not be separated. We were ordered onto the train, but given no direction about which car to board. Herr Thienelt and the front of our little chain said, "Straight ahead!" and we followed him. Herr Thienelt was the first one into our boxcar, and he pulled up Juergen. There were no stairs or ramp, and one had to rely on either upper body strength or help from those around you to hoist yourself up into the train.

I was next up, and while Juergen helped pull me up, I heard what sounded like an argument in German and Polish. Then there was a gunshot. When I was safely in the car, I could see the source of the commotion—an elderly man was lying face up on the platform, bleeding from his chest. The crowd instinctively moved away from the guard who had done the shooting. The guard did not seem to notice, but kept shouting out orders. Then, almost immediately, another shot rang out further down the line.

Juergen pulled Erica into the train and then helped mother, as the crowd surged forward to get into the train. We found our boxcar was already more than halfway filled with refugees from towns farther up the line. My family pressed against the wall that faced the platform. I could see out through a hole between the planks of wood. Every thirty seconds or so, another shot would ring out.

Right below me, a soldier grabbed an older woman who clearly had no chance of climbing onto the train unassisted and pulled her out of line. Instead of helping the old granny up onto the train, he pulled her out of the crowd and shot her in the back of the head. She was maybe twenty or thirty feet away from me and I heard her hit the pavement.

Another woman was carrying a tiny dog under her coat. It was the smallest dog I had ever seen. It literally would have fit in a purse and had skinny little legs like a chicken. As the lady set her dog up on the edge of our car, a guard seized the pet and shot it right there. The woman became hysterical and inconsolable and had to be dragged into our car by strangers.

When there was absolutely no more room in the boxcars, the door slid shut and the remaining refugees were ordered back into the train station. Our train sat there, not moving.

The woman's body that had been shot still lay there on the platform, as were a number of other bodies. I could see her clearly in the pale morning light. Her face was toward me and her eyes were still open. A mass of brain had been forced out of her nose. I had the uncanny sense she was watching me, even though I knew better. When I looked at her, I still saw someone with an inner life and her own thoughts.

After a personal eternity (about an hour), the train finally started to move. Those of us who were by the walls were lashed by the frigid air as the train gathered speed. The stench inside was horrible and there was nowhere for us to move or sit. There was not much to see, either. You could only see the coat of the person in front of you. The crowd staggered as the train swayed, and the car was so cramped, it was impossible to not be pressed awkwardly against strangers.

The train station had been so crowded. I assumed the entire town of Bad Dekova had been emptied of Germans. I overheard a woman who, between sobs, was telling someone the story about how she had to leave her grown daughter behind. The daughter had accepted a job working for the local government in order to stay behind. I knew Hedwig was probably working at that moment, and felt as bad as ever about leaving her behind.

After a few hours the smell in the train became unbearable, and I especially noticed the older people had a hard time breathing. The train kept going faster and faster and people started worrying where we might end up. The people in the train knew for sure it would not go to one of those concentration camps, where we knew so many small Jewish children lost their lives. Siberia, however, was a possibility.

After about an hour, the train slowed to a stop, but nobody opened the door. We heard footsteps on the roof of the boxcar. Mother speculated they were more Poles, intent on stealing whatever they could from us. They never showed themselves.

At about the time the train started up again, maybe thirty minutes later, another mother in our car realized her baby had died. She had not noticed the baby was not breathing, but she cried louder and longer than anyone else in our car for the rest of the journey. A man in the back started calling out to his mother, who was unconscious and who soon died. We were all cold, hungry, exhausted, and terrified.

It was noon by the time the train came to a stop. Mother told us not to get separated no matter what happened. The door slid open and the crowd instinctively drew back from it. A male voice addressed our car, answering a question I did not hear, "You have arrived in Broistedt. Please step out. Your trip is over."

I did not believe him, nor did the crowd, initially.

We had reached the West. One by one, however, the crowd started forward, climbing and jumping down from the boxcar. Herr Thienelt was the first of our party to climb out, and immediately helped the three of us and mother down.

I looked around. We were at another train station, this one even smaller than Bad Dakova's. The main building was, in fact, a kiosk on the covered platform. I looked back and about three or four people were lying on the wood planks. They were elderly and had not been strong enough to make the trip.

The man who announced the arrival was a German. We could see that. I was struck by the fact that, for the first time in months, we were not surrounded by armed guards anymore. German officials in civilian dress and coats stood by to make sure everyone was accounted for.

The German stood on a bench and directed the crowd to a small building near the station, where our arrival would be noted. Mother placed her hand firmly on my shoulder and guided me there. The disorganized crowd eventually filed into a line that led into the small building, a railway storage shed. We were near the end of the line and waited for more than two hours in the cold. Inside, two men sat at tables, taking the names of the families and issued bus tickets. When we reached the tables, the official said, "Family name?"

"Breitkopf and Thienelt," mother said.

The man looked up, confused. "All the same family?"

"No," Herr Thienelt chimed in. "But we have been traveling together."

"Well, we'll have to register you as separate families."

The other station opened up and Herr Thienelt stepped up to the other official and gave him his name. The official took a quick census of our family and any living arrangements we might be able to make, but we knew nobody in the area. He wrote our names down in a register, issued us bus tickets, temporary identification and housing assignment, and directed us toward our bus. It was parked in a row of busses in front of the station.

After we stepped out of the little shack, we realized Herr Thienelt's ticket had a different destination than ours. We were going to be taken to a home in Broistedt. Herr Thienelt's ticket was for Braunschweig, which was maybe twenty kilometers away. He asked for our new address and told us he would write to us that night. We boarded our bus. Within five minutes of pulling away from the station, we arrived at what would be our temporary home.

Following the war, Germans in the West were required to open their homes to refugees who had been deported. We were to be housed with an elderly couple, the Reinstadtlers, who lived in a big brick house that abutted a sugar factory. When Herr Reinstadtler opened the door, we introduced ourselves and explained that we had been told to report to their home. Herr Reinstadtler was thin, jowly and bald. Frau Reinstadtler was large, frumpy and nearly deaf. They welcomed us politely but without enthusiasm. We thanked them for their hospitality. They took us to a little room in the back of their flat where we would live for the next ten months.

The Reinstadtlers' home was rather dilapidated. Herr Reinstadtler explained they had used our room for storage and their son had only recently moved in a bed, sofa and a small table. The room had a high ceiling, and a single light bulb hung down on a string. The size of my room in Hummelstadt was not large enough for the four of us to live without constantly tripping over one another. This room was not as big. A sofa had been placed against the wall the building shared with the sugar factory. A small window at the back of the room let in a little light if we pulled back the flimsy floral curtain that framed it. There was a rusty old bed with a large mattress. The view showed the huge, brick factory. There was a small rug, but otherwise, the uneven wood floor was uncovered. Old wallpaper came apart from the wall at the ceiling, and as we made ourselves comfortable, we found there were holes in the wall behind the sofa. There was a small burner on the table where we could cook.

The room was very cold. A draft blew in from the window, which did not close all the way. Also, cold air seeped in from behind the sofa and through the floorboards. Mother, Erica and I would sleep in the bed, a king-sized mattress on a rusted iron frame, and Juergen would sleep on the hard, narrow antique sofa.

There was a communal bathroom at the other end of the house, near the washroom. The bathroom was a relic from an era long past. It had no running water. It was essentially an indoor out house. The stench was powerful and offensive, even though we poured lime or sand into the toilet after using it.

When I went in to examine the bathroom, a large rat sat on edge of the wooden toilet seat and stared at me. I shrieked. I did not wait to see if the rat had been startled, but ran back to mother. The rat was still there when I went back. Juergen flapped his coat at the rodent, and it jumped off the seat and disappeared into a corner.

Frau Reinstadtler came in and apologized about the rats. She said they had tried everything to keep them out, but they were drawn to the sugar in the warehouse next to us. The only thing that kept the rats at bay was the family's yappy toy poodle. She invited us into the kitchen for a meal of bacon and warm biscuits. I didn't realize how hungry I was and how long it had been since we had a hot meal. I ate so fast, thinking back at the time during the war when I had to go hungry for so long.

This house in which we stayed was perpetually cold during March. One morning not long after we arrived, we were at breakfast with the Reinstadtler's when Frau Reinstadtler remarked that a train loaded with coal would be passing through town that morning. Sometimes, they said, coal spilled out from the tops of the cars and could be found strewn along the tracks after the shipment passed through. They were too old to go lug coal around, so mother volunteered my siblings and me.

Later, we bundled up and set out on our mission. The train station was so close we could walk to the tracks easily. When we arrived, a number of people had already showed up for scrounging. After an hour, however, the train had not yet arrived, and people began to go home. Juergen decided we would wait and we would not go home empty-handed. So he told us to search the tracks for any coal that maybe had been dropped earlier. We hunted alongside the tracks away from the station, assuming we had a better chance of finding coal away from the station. We walked down about a kilometer and found a few lumps, which we put in the sled the Reinstadtler's had given us to transport the coal.

We kept on searching, moving farther and farther away from the town, convinced that we would find more. After about an hour of walking and kicking up new snow, we heard the rumble of a train coming down the tracks. We were alone, quite far away from the station now. When the engine came into sight, it was moving slowly enough that it would probably not spill much coal.

Without warning, as the open cars rolled passed us, Juergen stepped up to the train and grabbed a hold of a ladder on the side of one of the cars. I screamed out of fear and admiration, and Erica and I ran alongside the car as Juergen climbed to the top of the car. At the top, he reached in and started throwing pieces of coal over his shoulder. We let the coal sit there for the moment and followed alongside the car as coal rained down around us. When he thought he had thrown enough to fill the sled, Juergen carefully climbed down the ladder and paused. He checked to make sure he would not collide with anything and carefully jumped off the train and tumbled in the snow.

When he got up, he was trembling. He had been terrified of falling off. "Did you get it?" he asked, and then ordered, "Get it!" He was afraid someone had seen him stealing from the train and wanted to get out of there before any police came. Also, I think, he was so full of adrenaline he could not keep still.

Erica and I loaded the coal into the sled. It was dirty and blackened our gloves. Juergen was much dirtier from having climbed onto the train. We hid the extra coal among the trees and brush lining the tracks, where we could find it easily in the future.

We walked home dragging the sled behind us. The coal was covered with canvas sacks we brought. When we arrived at the house, Erica announced to mother we had been successful and recounted the story of how Juergen had leaped onto the train. Mother, however, was angry at Juergen and scolded him for doing something so careless and stupid. "You could have been crushed!" she yelled. We had not considered that at the time. It had seemed like such a natural thing for Juergen to do, and he had done it so easily.

***

Now that we had a permanent address, Mother decided that we would return to school. We had been out of school for about a year, and if it hadn't been for Herr Thienelt's attention and tutoring over that time, we would have fallen too far behind to continue with students our own age.

Mother made arrangements and we started school about a week after we arrived in Broistedt. It was a short distance away from the house and we walked each day to school through the gloomy town. Broistedt was a dirty place of about seven thousand people. The town had not had the money or manpower to maintain itself during the war, and the streets showed signs of disrepair.

Erica and I were placed in a class with other ten-year olds at the local public school. Public school was a change from our old private school. We noticed an overwhelming lack of nuns on the staff. We enjoyed being back among other students, though we didn't know anybody or make many friends. There was only this one girl we knew. She was from Bad Dekova, and we became good friends with her pretty soon. Her name was Gunhilde, and she was in the same class with us. Most of these kids had been friends for years, and we stuck out as recent arrivals to the town. Even though we were surrounded by children our age, Erica and I still felt alone.

Although we were able to continue at the grade level we should have been, it was only through hard work and mother and Juergen's help that we were able to pass all of our classes. If we failed two subjects, we would be held back for one year.

The workload was really quite remarkable, considering our age. Erica and I would rise at 6:00 every morning and quiz each other on our subjects. One of the more brutal aspects of the curriculum was the inevitable "pop quiz." The teachers were encouraged, I believe, to make life as difficult for students as possible. It was not uncommon for three or even four teachers to give us tests on the same day. There was a two-hour break during the middle of the day, during which we either ate the lunches we brought or went home for Mittagessen. (The school had no cafeteria).

Every night we had homework, which we did at the little table in our room. Juergen would do his work on the sofa, and when we were having problems, he would help us.

I thought this new life living in Broistedt wasn't really the best conditions to live in, but at least it was a home. Four of us lived in one room. I didn't complain, but I was still remembering living in my parent's big mansion which was once my home. I won't forget it for the rest of my life. I was missing Hedwig again and was wondering if she would still be alive.

Thienelt came down to visit several times during the week, and he would also tutor us. Father's lawyer friend became a sort of constant presence during this time, and he and mother grew increasingly close. By the time he visited us during the second week of our stay, he had already found himself a position in a law office in Braunschweig. He had a lot of work, but he made time to come down and visit us, nonetheless.

Actually, he was visiting mother more than anyone else, and we could see our mother grow more and more fond of him. Occasionally, Herr Thienelt would take us out for a movie. There was a movie house in Lebenstedt, which was about fifteen kilometers away. Erica and I often went there alone by bus on weekends. Herr Thienelt also made time on Sundays to take Juergen to the local soccer field, where Juergen spent most of his free time.

After a few weeks, and perhaps sensing some competition from Herr Thienelt for his wife's affection, father began to visit us regularly, usually on weekends. He was working steadily now and had even build up a new law practice in Hildesheim. It was next to his apartment across from the train station, a great location for walk-in business. He always brought a bag of food with him filled with fruit, sausage, bread and butter. This was our main source of food for the week.

Mother's affair with Thienelt might not have grown as it had, if we had been able to join my father in Hildesheim. It had been more subtle in Hummelstadt, but their romance had blossomed once we had been shipped to the West.

Father tried very hard to find a place for us to live in Hildesheim, but that was impossible. Most large cities and towns had been bombed so heavily during the war, there was a severe housing shortage, even in Hildesheim. This was why we and so many other Germans who had been shipped in from the East were deposited in insignificant little towns across the countryside; they had escaped virtually all bombing, unless of course there had been resistance when the armies had come through. As a result, there were no apartments large enough for our family in Hildesheim, and certainly nothing as big as what had been accustomed to in Hummelstadt. For these reasons, my parents decided it would be best for the family to remain separated a little while longer, while father searched for a new home.

By the beginning of the summer, mother no longer met father at the railway station, but sent the children to get him. At this point, even I realized something had happened to their marriage, though I could not say exactly what.

Once when we picked father up, he had brought us very pretty dresses, which he had picked out himself. I loved the colors and the way the dresses were made. These were sophisticated styles and their cut made us look much older. We loved them, but mother disapproved strongly when we showed them to her. Father did not see any problem with the dresses—-we were, after all, almost eleven and he thought we would appreciate them. Mother said we were too young for those dresses and she would do all of the clothes shopping.

Father's response to this proclamation was anger. He shouted at my mother for what I believed was the first time in his life: "Damn it, Wally, they're my daughters, too! If I want to spoil them every so often, I will." Mother told him to get out. We would see him next week, but she was too angry and might say something she'd regret. Father put on his hat and left.

Erica, Juergen and I were stunned. We had never witnessed such a fight between them before. I started to cry and mother snapped, "Quiet. You're not ready for those clothes." In fact, we probably were. We were growing up.

We were starting to notice boys and hoped they noticed us. Whether she knew it or not, mother was trying to keep us from getting any older. She insisted on holding onto the little girls she raised in Hummelstadt. She was, in fact, pushing us away.

***

As the months passed, the rodent situation in the Reinstadtlers' house became increasingly dire. For a while, my family assigned the little poodle, Strolch, to the role of bathroom monitor. The dog would protect us from any rats or mice that might venture into the bathroom when it was occupied.

Initially, Strolch found the thrill of the chase exhilarating, and we would only have to ask him, "Do you want...?" and he would know immediately what to do. He would even offer to show us the way. This amused us greatly. At least until the rats found out that Strolch was more prone to bark than bite. After a few weeks, the rats would become aggressive and attack the poor pup. We eventually had to stop him from going into the bathroom, because when he returned, his legs would be scratched and bitten and bleeding. Strolch, a smart little poodle, perhaps was sensing he had been shamed on the field of battle. Still, he eagerly sought out confrontations with the rodents.

One day in the spring, mother was peeling potatoes in the little washroom next to the bathroom, when she heard a noise behind her. She turned to greet what she thought was Strolch, but was in fact a pair of large rats. Mother yelped and Strolch came tearing through the door and bit down on one of the rats' tails. The two rodents scampered out of the washroom with Strolch in pursuit.

Mother came down to our room and told us that Strolch had redeemed himself. She showed us Strolch's rather disgusting trophy, the severed, bald tail. After that, Strolch was allowed to resume his duties. He would wait in the hall beside the bathroom for visitors.

It was after a particularly scary trip to the bathroom that Erica came back, crying out of frustration. Erica seemed to be in a very bad mood. Maybe she didn't get enough sleep the night before, as we understood, because the bed we had to share with mother was everything but comfortable.

She began to moan piteously about what had happened to us, "We are kicked out of our house and forced to leave everything behind. They come and take us in the middle of the night and don't tell us where we're going, and then we're shipped off to a town where I don't want to be and forced to live in a smelly old room with people who don't know us or even like us. I HATE IT SO MUCH. I HATE IT!" She pounded her fist on the bed and screamed.

Actually, Juergen felt the same way. It seemed like an especially cruel trick we had arrived at the place where we were at that moment. What we all really needed was a pep talk from our mother, but she was not going to play ball.

"Do you how lucky we are, Erica?" she sneered in an accusing voice. "Did you see what happened to those people in the train station? That could have been any one of us." She trembled with anger. "Despite all of this, nobody in our family has died. What about the people who lost everything, including their families? I honestly don't know what we did to deserve to be so lucky, Erica."

It was at this point that Mother reminded us again to think about all of the Jewish people who were murdered during the war. This was the second time she spoke about the Holocaust, and more in detail. When I found out about it for the first time, I just couldn't believe it.

Erica and I had largely been shielded from the Holocaust, a national embarrassment to this day. It was something so horrible and so vast, mother could not even describe it to us. My sister and I attributed the sense of embarrassment about the Holocaust to having been defeated, when at the same time we were constantly being reassured by mother and Herr Thienelt we were going to be okay and were safe to the end.

Juergen was a little savvier about what had happened; that little demon Juris spoke about little else to him during the Goblinsky's stay in our mansion. But we twins knew very little when the news about the concentration camps came out after the war.

Mother reminded us again, "Do you know about all the experiments the Nazis did on twins under Dr. Joseph Mengele?" Mother asked. "He tried to join them back together. Or they'd poison one twin and then kill the other to see what was different. That could have been you, Erica. You are very, very lucky to be living in this house at all Erica, and don't you forget it. I never want to hear you complain about how inconvenienced you have been ever, ever again." Mother was at the point of tears as she ended her tirade. Suddenly, Erica had a very sad look on her face and she couldn't help crying. My own tears were dropping down from my eyes. It reminded me again of the terrible things Hitler had done to this world.

Juergen went back to his homework, while Erica and I contemplated what we had just heard, wondering if either of us would have lived.

***

One day, while we were studying with Herr Thienelt, he told mother a story about someone they had known in Hummelstadt who unexpectedly walked into his office in Braunschweig. During the occupation of the Poles, this woman was considered by most of the town to be a traitor. Herr Thienelt noted with some satisfaction she had been deported with the rest of her neighborhood. She said she wanted to divorce her husband. With great relish, he told mother how he had dressed her down in front of the staff and had pushed her out the door. "Tell your husband I'd be happy to help him draw up divorce papers," he had shouted as she stomped away.

By this time, mother and Herr Thienelt had obviously grown quite close. Father knew Herr Thienelt was spending a lot of time tutoring us, but he probably didn't realize how much time mother spent alone with Herr Thienelt. While his visits averaged about three times per week, mother would often go up to visit him during our school day. She was usually back before we got home.

If my sister and I had been a little older, we might have read more into the little signs of affection Thienelt and mother showed one another. Mother no longer referred to him as Herr Thienelt, but as Hans. He would place his arm around her or hold her hand as we went out to restaurants. I never saw them embrace. We were still quite young and did not yet understand the complexity of adult emotion. Besides, we loved Herr Thienelt, too. He was always there for us and we had accepted him as a member of the family while my father was away. He treated us as if we were his own. I think Juergen was a little more mature about the deepening relationship between Herr Thienelt and mother.

Mother was an independent woman, but she had always been faithful to father. She liked the attention of other male friends, but she always knew what she was doing. My parents would go on vacation together, but mother always made the decision where and for how long she wanted to go. My father, on the other hand, though reserved probably had had an affair or two before the war. Herr Thienelt most likely had been aware of this long before he came to stay with us, and I think, in a way, father's indiscretion served as a sort of justification for allowing himself to feel increasing affection for my mother. Mother was not naïve. She knew her husband had a propensity for wandering, but she always kept it to herself or confided in Hedwig.

Nonetheless, a deep affection between Herr Thienelt and mother was brewing. The only child sophisticated enough to perceive this by Juergen.

At some point, mother had to make a decision about her future--would she remain with my father or would she commit to Herr Thienelt?

That June, during one of my father's visits, mother announced her decision. The entire family had gone to a local restaurant for lunch. Father was talking about the trouble he was having finding a place for us all to live. "Honestly, there's nothing, not even nearby."

"That's not important," mother said. "I don't think I want to move back in, anyway."

"How's that?"

"I want a divorce. I'm not going into it now, Wolfgang, not in public. I'd appreciate it very much if you'd grant me it."

We were stunned, and did not know what to say or even if we should say anything. We could not imagine a life where mother and father were not in love, married or longing to be reunited. The meal, of course, was over.

The walk home was silent, and our parents dropped us off at the Reinstadtlers' while they went for a walk so they could talk about what mother had said.

Mostly, I remember pacing and rubbing my fingers together nervously while my parents were out. I cringed at the thought of a divorce, and when mother returned without father, I was almost relieved by her irritation.

"He said he would not grant me a divorce," she told Juergen, but we were all clearly meant to hear it. "We're going to stay married." And then she sat down on the couch and started to cry. She hadn't mentioned Herr Thienelt to father.

Mother explained that father did not want to risk losing his children. This satisfied us enough at the time. In fact, the truth was more complicated and less endearing. Father had never been good with the money he earned. He could not manage it. He didn't know how to invest in stocks. Mother did, and he relied on her to do these things for him. He depended on her, and would have been in a weak position if she left him.

Now that she informed father she wanted a divorce, mother felt freer to express her fondness for Herr Thienelt. For the rest of June and July, mother began visiting Herr Thienelt more often than she did father. Herr Thienelt's trips to Broistedt also became more frequent. He was getting skinny, but he and mother seemed happy, even though the children felt awkward in the presence of their open affection.

In early October, Mother started to get severe cramps. She said it was probably from stress or that she had a stomach ache. Later that week, however, we came home from school and found mother in bed, curled up in agony. Her sheets were bloody from the waist down. Frau Reinstadtler said she had called my father in Braunschweig, and he was coming down as soon as possible. She looked pale and could barely get a word out. Father arrived later that evening on the train, and said he had arranged for the doctor to come. When he arrived, we were stunned to see Dr. Heartel standing before us. Dr. Heartel had contacted my father shortly after he had been deported to the West. He was currently living in another nearby town called Harsum.

We waited outside while Dr. Heartel examined her. Mother was having a miscarriage, and she had lost a lot of blood. Usually, a miscarriage took care of itself, he said. She had some complications, in that she had not expelled all of the tissue. He had been able to remove it without surgery, and he would stay the night with us to make sure her bleeding had stopped.

Father did not know that mother was pregnant. I imagine he assumed it was his. He had tried to restore a bit of romance to their marriage after mother asked for the divorce. He was upset to hear that she had miscarried.

I don't know if she knew she was pregnant, but I suspect she did. I have since wondered if mother thought a pregnancy from another man might secure a divorce, but she never spoke about it. Father left the next day. Dr. Heartel described mother's prognosis as good even though she lost a good deal of blood and was weak.

My mother stayed in bed for about a week after Dr. Heartel left. As she recuperated, she was able to spend longer and longer periods out of bed. During this time, she was constantly attended by Herr Thienelt.

Then, one day, when she resumed her schedule, Hans failed to show up, despite a promise he made the day before. Mother was worried and when he did not show up the next morning, she took the next train up to Braunschweig to see him.

When we came home that evening, Mother was not there. Frau Reinstadtler told us where she had gone and that she would be back soon.

When she returned, Mother was in a sort of shock and sat down on the bed. "Herr Thienelt is in the hospital and is very sick," she said. Having said it out loud, she started to cry. I sat with her on the bed. "What happened?" Juergen asked.

Mother explained that she had arrived at his apartment that morning, but she could not get an answer at his door. So, she knocked on the door of a neighbor, who told her that Herr Thienelt had been taken to the hospital that morning.

When she arrived at the hospital, Herr Thienelt was in bed talking to his sister Barbara, who had come to be with him. The doctors diagnosed him with colon cancer. It had already spread to other organs by the time he had shown any symptoms. He was dying.

Mother spent Herr Thienelt's last few weeks with him in the hospital. She came home every night and told us how he was doing. He had good days and bad ones, but as her reports got progressively worse, even I could see how bad it was. He was on powerful painkillers and was slipping away.

During the last week, at the end of November, mother sent for father, who came down to attend Herr Thienelt's funeral. At this point, I think father realized how close mother and Herr Thienelt were, and he accepted it gloomily. He was very sad, too. Herr Thienelt had been his close and trusted friend for a long time, and found it hard to be anything but distraught as he died. He was frustrated and sighed heavily as he helped us with our homework. Mother came home then.

She gave us the news that Herr Thienelt had died that afternoon. "His family was there and was able to say goodbye." Throughout the ordeal, Herr Thienelt's two brothers and sister had kept a vigil by his side, and one or more of them was always there whenever mother visited.

Father stayed until we went to the grave site in Braunschweig a few days later. A small group, mostly his family, assembled at the graveyard for the service. It was my first funeral, and I remember how lonely everybody looked. The Breitkopf's: mother, father, Erica, Juergen and I, stood together and prayed and wept.

Chapter Nine: Life After Death

It is an awful feeling to think that someone's death brought our family back together. Actually, in a way that's what happened. I am certain that if Herr Thienelt had not died, my mother would have been granted a divorce. She was so certain of this that she and Herr Thienelt had already bought an apartment building near Berlin and planned to rent out the rooms. My siblings and I had no idea of this.

Mr. Thienelt was also accepting us children as his own, as mother told me. I could understand now how my mother must have felt. Her whole personality had changed already during the war. After everything that had happened to mother in the last two years, Herr Thienelt's death finally broke her spirit. She spent the next few months essentially in mourning.

She was not sleeping soundly at night and often slept through the day. She no longer had anyone visit while we were at school. It was difficult to convince her to leave the room, and the only way we ever got her outside was through badgering, which didn't make things any better. She often snapped at us for no reason and insisted we spend more and more time with her. Erica and I were torn, because we, too, missed Herr Thienelt, and understood how awful she felt. At the same time, Erica and I were growing up and increasingly longed for our independence, or at least to enjoy ourselves.

Father came and visited us regularly over the next several months, trying to keep mother's spirits up. He was exactly the wrong person for this job, however. He reminded her of all she had lost, and it seemed to her as if she would never escape her suffering. I do think she appreciated the effort, though.

Also, in deference to the children's wishes to roam a little more widely, he would take one or two of us to Hildesheim for a weekend. He always left at least one of us at home to be with mother.

In early April, father asked mother to come up to Hildesheim. He said he wanted her opinion before signing the papers for an apartment he was interested in buying. When she arrived, it was clear the apartment was not intended solely for him. It had two very small bedrooms and had tall raftered ceilings, since it was on the top floor. His invitation was a not-so-subtle offer for the family to move back in with him. Mother approved of the apartment for her children, and she agreed to live in Hildesheim. Erica's eyes lit up hearing this good news, as she hated that smelly, dumpy room where we lived in Broistedt. I was also happy, as something new always excited me.

We arrived in Hildesheim in the middle of April, after father signed the papers and had a chance to move in some furniture, which he was able to buy from one of his clients. The train ride to Hildesheim revealed a world in bloom, and the pleasure I took in its beauty was augmented by the happiness of being reunited as a family. We girls were very excited about having our own place again. We were at the age where we were developing new interests; we were no longer children. We looked forward to becoming young women and the freedoms it offered.

Mother was still gloomy and cried a lot. I suspect she thought this move to be something of a defeat for her.

When we arrived at Vionville Strasse eighteen, our new address, we all ran up the stairs to see the apartment. The main room was spacious and its tall, sloped ceiling added an illusion of extra space to the room. We liked the furniture father had found for our living room I thought it was ready for entertaining. The rest of the apartment was more sparsely furnished. My sister and I picked the smallest of the two bedrooms for our own, since it was the most quiet. Not only would we be able to study without distraction there, but it also overlooked a nice, little park with a beautiful view.

With about hundred thousand residents, Hildesheim was larger than any town we had lived in. Still, it made me so sad to see how much damage the war had done to so many beautiful cities. Hildesheim was heavily damaged by air raids.

Before it had been bombed, Hildesheim had been one of the most beautiful, small cities in Germany. It was home to a thousand year-old rosebush in the Cathedral cloisters. That is thought to be world's oldest living rose. Today it continues to flourish.

The church was partly destroyed during the war, but the roots of the bush remained and the blossoms came back. I was thinking back how much I missed our beautiful rose garden in our mansion, a garden where the water trickled down to a huge, concrete fountain surrounded by so many roses in different colors. The local nickname for the town was "The City in Green," no doubt a reference to the pristine countryside between Hildesheim and Hanover. The closest largest city was Hanover, which was about twenty five kilometers away. It was a shame that Hildesheim had been bombed; a couple of the buildings on our street had been ruined by Allied raids. Also, many of the civilians we met had been directly affected by the bombing. Many of our new schoolmates had family members who had been killed by bombing. We knew many people in Hummelstadt who had lost family in the war, but we had never experienced the fury or grave aftermath of aerial bombardment.

Within a week or so of our arrival, mother began to interview potential maids. She finally settled on a chubby blond girl by the name of Gisela. She was about twenty three or so, and had lost her home to bombing. As part of the arrangement, Gisela would live with us, but she would sleep on a sofa bed in our small kitchen, more like a scullery maid in an old English house rather than a member of the family, as Hedwig had been.

We often wondered what happened to Hedwig, though Mother avoided the subject. She did not want to contemplate what might have happened to her. Having loved and been reared by Hedwig, we were never really close to Gisela. She was pleasant and shy, and her job entailed mostly cleaning and cooking, which she did slowly and steadily.

Mother reassumed responsibility of raising us for the time being; we were older now and did not need perpetual supervision. We would walk through the city to school by ourselves every morning, which was only about fifteen minutes away. We varied our route home as often as we could, since it was usually the only part of the day we had to ourselves.

In the spring, with the warm sun shining down on us, Erica and I would sit in the park near our house after school and discuss which assignments we would do first. Often we would watch families walking by with their children realizing how many small Jewish children had also lost their lives in those gas chambers in the concentration camps, and how many others had been killed by bombing or froze to death while being forced from their homes. Sometimes, we met Juergen there, who would either be camped out on the grass with a magazine or book or kicking around a soccer ball with some of his new classmates around the meticulously tended park.

I just didn't realize the sheer randomness of aerial bombing. Since so much time had passed, I witnessed bizarre juxtapositions of devastation and charm that I would have never seen in Hummelstadt.

On one block, one side of the street had been reduced to shattered stone and timbers, while across the road the houses were unscathed except for shattered windows, most of which had been patched with cardboard. On another block, the only building hit had been an elementary school.

On rare occasions, we would find our path blocked by a police barricade. An unexploded bomb had been found in some overlooked cranny, and the block had to be cleared while the bomb was removed.

***

In Hildesheim, during the six-week summer break from school, Erica and I got reacquainted with our father. He was out of the house for most of the day, but he closed his office from 1 to 3 p.m. (as was the custom in Germany) to come home for Mittagessen. At mother's request, he brought home cuts of meat and sausages from the butcher shop that was next door to the office. After eating, he would take a nap in the living room, until Gisela brought him his cup of coffee and he returned to work. Depending on how many clients he had, he would return home at 6 p.m. or later.

***

That summer, Mother tried to invite some people over for the evening. It was only a small get-together with some of her friends she used to invite in Hummelstadt. The gaiety of the parties she used to hold was not the same for the children, nor apparently, for mother. The few parties she threw were much more basic than the ones she used to host. In the first place, they were held in our living room, and without a ballroom, a band and a fleet of hired staff, the parties more closely resembled a meeting than my mother's old parties, and I realized how a war had change everything.

The guests were typically members of our extended family, including my aunt Kaete and grandmother, with whom we had been reunited through a charity. They had moved into a small apartment in Hildesheim (they came over every week anyway to take a bath since they had no bathtub). There was really only one distinguished person that would come to these parties--the wife of one of Herr Thienelt's brothers was a famous dancer at the time. She would arrive in a long, white flowing dress wearing a huge hat and heels, but there was no room for her to entertain or no music for her to dance to. The guests mostly sat around with drinks, talking mostly about what the terrible war had done to so many people.

One lady knew people who lived in Nemmesdorf, close to the city Koenigsberg. The Red Army invaded this village with tanks in 1944. When they were fleeing West on foot they had to cross a bridge. She described how the Russians had damaged this bridge and horses pulling wagons all plunged into the water. People were screaming. Some managed to get out, but most lost their lives.

We also heard the true story about the boat Wilhelm Gustloff loaded with several thousand refugees and how the Russians had sunk this boat. Hundreds died in that cold water in 1945.

I remember a widowed friend of my mother's. After a couple drinks, she would burst into tears. Her only daughter decided to remain behind and marry one of the Polish occupiers. She didn't know if or when she would see her again. The new addresses of mutual friends who had been relocated exchanged hands. These were somber, low-key affairs, and my sister and I made plans to be elsewhere when these parties were thrown. We were still not really invited guests, anyway.

***

Mother attributed her dissatisfaction with her parties to the size of our apartment. She began almost immediately scouting Hildesheim for a new place for us to live, somewhere where she would be able to entertain more guests. After many disappointing searches, she came across a property not far from our current home. She was so excited about the new place she took Erica and me along to see it before she bought it, something an impassive businesswoman like my mother would normally not do. In a way, it made me happy when I did see mother coming alive again. Even if she showed her enthusiasm to us, I could tell she was still so sad inside from suffering so much during the war.

We walked to the new house because it was a private street and mother said the guard who worked at the gate was rather zealous in his duties. The building itself had three stories, with an attractive and spacious balcony that wrapped around the second floor. From the stairwell, one stepped into a small coatroom and then through a door into a long hallway with access to all of the different rooms.

We toured the house as mother happily babbled on about the hardwood floors and high ceilings. We looked at a couple of the extra bedrooms, the pick of which, mother promised us. She led us into the room she proposed for Father's private office. It was at the back of the house and was lined with built-in bookcases. It had a nice fireplace trimmed with a glass mosaic interlace and the windows afforded a fantastic view of the property's lake. On the shore, we saw a swan was sitting on her nest. Small decorative mosaics were found throughout the house, which caught the light that streamed in from the large windows and added color, sparkle, and life to the home.

There were three large rooms on the second floor, which were joined by elegant sliding doors that could be opened for the parties. Mother was imagining and anticipating exclusively for her parties.

After that outing, we could finally see mother's excitement, but it didn't mean she had forgotten all the bad experiences of the war. There was hardly a day when I didn't hear my parents still talking about it.

We children were mostly pleased by the thought of not having to transfer to a new school and by having a private swimming pool. (Later, we would spend so much time in it that father would refer to us as fishes). We raved about the house to our father that night, and after consulting with mother, he agreed to see it the next day. When they returned, they had signed the lease and announced we could move in at the beginning of the month.

Mother soon set about filling the house with furnishings fit for a grand and beautiful space. Her proudest purchase was a long, intricately carved table and matching chairs for the dining room and father's new grand piano.

As soon as we moved in, Erica and I wanted to invite some girls from school over to show off a little and cement our relationships with them. Mother said that the house was not yet ready, and she would be the one who would throw the first party.

As soon as the new house was ready, she threw one of her parties. This was more like the ones she had in Hummelstadt, with many people, lavish food and good entertainment. We were amazed how many people we recognized from the parties in Hummelstadt. It seemed by then, people started allowing themselves to enjoy life again, even if only for an evening. Mother did everything she could to create a relaxed atmosphere, almost making herself mad in the pursuit. These were the types of parties Erica and I could take an interest in. Erica would get excited at the prospect of playing her accordion for the guests and would practice a few songs before upcoming parties, in case she was asked to perform.

I remember her playing "Lila Marlene," a universal song during the war. Everybody knew it. This was my sister's favorite song. The lyrics describe the sad story about two people in love during the war and how they were hoping to see each other again in front of a lantern after the war was over. After the war, this song brought many sad memories to so many women. Mother insisted I sing for her guests, and I usually performed operettas by Handel or Johann Strauss to father's piano accompaniment. Often I had dreamed of becoming a singer one day, but dancing was still my priority.

In order to prepare her children for such home entertaining when we were older, she enrolled us in piano lessons. Juergen was the only one who pursued the piano into adulthood. I simply found it a distraction from more important homework.

Even though Erica and I were only about fifteen or so, Mother was already busy trying to introduce us to young men she thought would make good husbands. It was no secret of her intentions to select suitable husbands for her daughters. The best candidates, she thought, were the sons of her friends. We had no objection to meeting her friends' sons, but we nonetheless planned to make those choices by ourselves when the time came.

For some reason, mother started buying us a lot of formalwear. Erica and I accepted the clothes, but wondered what she was up to. As it turned out, she intended to introduce us to society. The way to do this, it seemed, was for mother to take us to public performances once a week (operas, plays, and symphonies mostly) and to introduce us to her friends during the intermission.

Occasionally, we were introduced to potential suitors who happened to "stop by" the house to visit. Mother hoped to pair me off with a well-known professor from Bonn. I still remember Dr. Wessing, a pale, pasty, unkempt little genius who was about twelve years older than me. I was disgusted and embarrassed by this older man's obvious interest in me. I was in no way ready to date someone that old. After he left, I accused my mother of trying to sell me off as a child bride, which I thought was nothing she'd ever do. Mother paid no attention to my protests. She often said we were too young to understand and it was for the best. I resolved never to take one of the suitors mother arranged for me seriously. She continued to try to pass me off onto older men, but whenever one was invited to our home, I counted the minutes until he left.

***

Mother took Juergen's imminent departure for college hard. Juergen was destined to study law, like his father, because our parents insisted. In an effort to recapture her children's waning youth, mother purchased a second home in the Bavarian town of Garmisch-Partenkirchen, where the entire family would all be able to spend time together during summer and winter vacations.

We arrived in a slow train, in an air-conditioned sleeper car. All of the buildings in this little town looked the same by law. They were mostly low, two-story whitewashed stone buildings, and were adorned with balconies and flowerboxes. In a way, Garmisch-Partenkirchen was the perfect town for a summer/winter home. This section of the Bavarian Alps, at the southern border of Germany, is known for its skiing in the winter and hiking in the summer.

Close to it was another beautiful resort area called Berchtesgaden. It was in this area that Hitler's Eagle's Nest was built, perched atop a mountain. I do remember passing his villa by car one time. It looked like the rest of the houses in Bavaria.

The tallest peak in Germany, at almost ten thousand feet, is near Garmisch-Partenkirchen, called the Zugspitze. To get to the Zugspitze, we would take a train, then transfer to a cable car, and finally walk to the ski lift. Many people took the cable car to the Schneeferner Haus, an elegant restaurant and lodge perched precariously on the mountain slopes. Sometimes Erica and I would rent snowshoes there and hike the rest of the way up the mountain.

On our first trip to the Zugspitze, the family planned to do some skiing, but my sister and I needed a few lessons before we could go as a family. After a few lessons, we were ready to join the family on the slopes, even though everyone else pulled ahead of us pretty quickly.

On my first day on the slopes, my family and I got off of the ski lift and approached the beginning of a long, straight ski run, the perfect place for a beginner like me. I could go straight, but was still learning how to slow down and turn. I pushed off and let gravity take over. Before I knew it, I was flying down the hill faster than I had ever gone on a bicycle. I was simultaneously thrilled and terrified, and I worked very hard at keeping my skis straight.

I coasted for several hundred yards, and as the slope leveled off, I turned the tips of my skis inward as I had been taught and slowed down. My family, however, had no intention of slowing down and they shouted for me to hurry as they zipped past. So I carefully pushed on to the edge of the next hill. Juergen, mother and father were all at the bottom by the time Erica and I reached the top. This slope was a little too steep for beginners, I thought, but we were on the easiest run on the mountain. About half way down the slope, for no apparent reason, I found myself tumbling down the hill. One ski pole flew away, then the other, and I was face down in the snow laughing hysterically. I was lying in my own debris field of ski equipment. I lost my hat, a glove, as well as both skis and poles. I gathered my equipment and my pride, got the skis on, and continued down to the bottom. At the bottom, Juergen, who had been left behind to wait for us, was laughing. "You looked like you exploded," he said, and we both burst into laughter.

***

Juergen's departure for college brought with it a new measure of freedom for my sister and me. A few months after Juergen had left for Freiburg, he called us and invited us up. He had joined a fraternity there and his friends were looking for dates for the winter ball. We were thrilled——a real college party.

The next day after school, Erica and I were off to Freiburg. Juergen met us at the train station. He gave us a tour of the campus, and the limitless opportunities that college seemed to represent seduced me. It showed me how limited my prospects were if I followed the path mother was setting for me.

Mother had approved to our dating Juergen's friends, assuming the boys were similar to Juergen——just the type of boys she would have us meet. The boys we met were fun and probably a bit more rowdy than mother would have approved of. The fraternity had pooled its money together and had rented a large hall for its ball, complete with a stocked bar and a band. I had never been drunk before, and I did not drink during our first visit to the Freiburg parties. As I got to know the guys in the fraternity (and had Juergen's assurance they would treat me like their sister), I felt more at ease.

The Freiburg parties were spirited affairs, and one of the few times

I felt like I was an integral part of a group, and was not ashamed to be myself. Often, the guys and their dates would take turns entertaining the crowd on stage, telling jokes, dancing, or playing an instrument. These sometimes spontaneously turned into talent competitions for a bottle of champagne. I remember on one occasion, the fraternity brothers selected four girls at random to sing. Arbitrarily, I found myself on stage with three other girls. I chose a song from Lehar's The Merry Widow and won the competition! I was also very proud to have won the first place in dancing the tango in a different competition. It was extremely gratifying to win the approval of my peers like that. That bottle of champagne was another adverse symbol in conforming to my mother's expectations.

At next party, however, I unexpectedly embarrassed myself, though I'm sure now nobody really cared or even noticed. During the party, someone called for a waltz, and it seemed everybody knew exactly what to do. My sister and I had no idea how to waltz. We had seen it before at mother's parties, but had never participated in the dance or had been taught. Of course, when we returned home the next day, I immediately told mother I wanted to learn how to dance. Mother, realizing this was one area of our formal education she had neglected, immediately enrolled my sister and me in dance lessons.

Dance lessons, in those days, were much more common among young adults than they are now. The course we took lasted about eight weeks and was run by a husband and wife team. The classes were held in a hall they rented big enough for many teens to dance in. The wife and husband would show us the steps while an assistant played the piano. Lessons lasted about three hours. We danced almost the entire time, going over and over the same steps time and again. Mother had heard this school had a good reputation, and she saw distinct advantages in having her daughters learn even more of the formal social graces.

The way the course was set up, however, it was also sort of a mixer for teens. This arrangement allowed my sister and me to meet boys that mother would probably otherwise forbid us from meeting.

Adhering to the age-old tradition, the boys selected their dancing partners at the beginning of each class. After a few weeks, a number of couples spontaneously came together, and you could tell who was going to pick you. I found myself repeatedly asked to dance by a boy named Wolfdieter. He was tall and handsome and very polite. The night after we first danced, I felt an electric tingle throughout my body, the overwhelming and pleasant sensation of an enormous crush. I was impatient and anxious at the same time for the next class. When that night finally arrived, to my delight, he asked me to dance, and from then on we were a couple.

He was a graceful dancer and good humored about my leaden, uncooperative feet. A hundred times, I just wanted to sink into his arms, but the formality of the class would not allow it. As the weeks went on and we got to know one another better, I was apprehensive that I would not have the chance to see him again. So we began to make dates to see one another outside of class. Mother knew nothing about these meetings. I was so excited, I told Gisela about him on the condition that she did not tell my mother.

Erica took vicarious pleasure in my happiness and suggested that I tell mother about Wolfdieter. She would sweeten mother to the deal by telling her about Wolfdieter's family. His father was, in fact, a prominent physician in Hildesheim and there seemed to me no reason why she might object to at least meeting him. I gave Erica permission to tell mother, and she was intrigued by Erica's description. She agreed to invite him over for coffee so she could look him over.

The resulting meeting was one of my most excruciating and disheartening embarrassments. Mother and Wolfdieter met not long after the dancing lessons ended. Wolfdieter was dressed very respectably. In my eyes he could do no wrong, and I was certain he would win mother over as he had won me over.

In any event, the informal coffee get together felt much like a police interrogation. I watched him fidget and cower behind his pastry as mother bombarded him relentlessly with questions about his family and education. He did his best under the circumstances, the dear boy, but when mother broke off the conversation, suddenly remembering an appointment, I knew the jury was back and the sentence would be severe.

What had sealed Wolfdieter's fate, in her eyes, was his age. It was nothing he had said. He was not finished with his education yet, and was only as old as I was. She forbade me to see him again. Most cruelly, she said if he was a few years older, he might do. I was heartbroken and enraged and refused to let my mother finish. I stomped off to my room and swore and cried.

Of course, I saw him again. Mother could not have kept me from him had she locked me in a closet. He became my first serious boyfriend. He called often (there was little mother could do to stop that), and we arranged to meet at the public swimming pool or go to movies together, where we had our first kiss. In the evenings, I would say I was going to study with a friend and then I would head straight to wherever Wolfdieter and I planned to meet. Our romance was, like most first loves, intense and brief. We were friends for years after that, and I always secretly believed that we might have been happy together.

***

Because we had graduated from high school and performed well on our exit exams, in the fall of 1953, Erica and I began attending college in Hanover. We enrolled in a four-year program in liberal arts. The campus was like no other we had ever been to.

The open air and freedom all the space suggested was seductive, and I looked forward to the walk to class every day. It was lovely and intimate. Some days, we would bring our lunch, or we have a picnic next to the pond at the edge of campus.

We took required classes, and, for the first time, electives. Mother had a definite idea about which classes we should choose, and since she was footing the bill, we generally took them. I knew I wanted to major in history, but in hindsight, the most important classes we took there were language classes in English and French. Mother insisted we take language.

In her first year, Erica took the hardest English class she could, and it was during this class she made her first contact with an American pen pal named James. Erica and James became fast friends through their letters. James was an airline mechanic in St. Louis, and his letters were full of invitations for Erica to visit him. She declined, explaining that her education came first. Maybe they would meet after she finished, she suggested. Erica kept up her correspondence with James throughout college.

***

One morning late in our first year at Hannover, mother asked Erica and me if we would like to be in a movie. An article had run in the newspaper telling about a film that was being made nearby, and the producers were looking for twins to be extras. Mother had already taken the liberty to submit our photos, and we had been invited to appear in the movie. Erica and I were very excited. We loved the movies and had our favorite actors. It seemed too good to be true to be invited to work on a movie. Erica asked mother if she would be coming with us. Mother said she wouldn't. A chartered bus would pick up the extras and bring them home each night for five days. We would need five different outfits apiece, for which we were responsible.

On the first morning of the shoot, we rose early and hurried down to breakfast. I asked mother what we could expect, but she had no idea. The movie was called Du mein stilles Tal (You, My Quiet Village), and it starred Kurt Jürgens and Winnie Markus. Erica and mother both fancied Kurt Jürgens. While I thought he was a good actor, I was more excited about simply being on film than being in a film with him.

The bus waited for us down the block (it was unable to get past the guard). We boarded at 8 a.m. Looking around the bus, we were probably the youngest people boarding. We took our seats and in about an hour and a half we arrived at our destination, a well-preserved castle in the Harz Mountains that we had visited before with our parents. It overlooked a pristine lake, and when we pulled in, I had butterflies in my stomach. Someone came on the bus and told us all to meet inside the castle.

When we entered, we saw the hair and makeup people were set up there. We each took a seat with a makeup artist. I did not say a word, but beamed with a strange sort of pride as they did my hair and piled on more makeup than I had ever worn before. I looked over at Erica and she was getting the same treatment. A wardrobe person came over and approved our clothes. I was wearing a light green satin dress with white stripes.

We were led out to the set, where a party was being staged. They sat us near the principle actors and told us exactly what to do. When the camera rolled, the crowd made a lot of noise. When the director called cut, everybody was suddenly subdued.

I remember there was a lot of waiting around while they moved cameras and fiddled with the hot lights. I was surprised at how much time went in to every shot. That morning I would not have thought I would be bored on a movie set, but after the novelty of the cameras had worn off a little, I distracted myself by talking with the actors who were there.

Our lunches were brief, communal affairs, and that first day we had beef stew with bread and butter. We had about half an hour before we were needed again and we worked until late in the evening.

On the second day of the shoot, I was sitting in the makeup chair when the director came up to me, fuming about how my hair looked. He talked about me as if I was not even there, and I felt awkward at the occasion how he talked to me; not approving my hair the way it was fixed exactly the same way it was done the day before.

What was I supposed to do? Why was he angry at me?

I felt awful for the woman doing my hair, but in the end, the director said it would be okay. I thought he needed to relax a little bit or maybe be a little more polite about it. At any rate, his energy over the five days we were there was impressive. He had so much to do, he may have gained the right to be a little cranky.

At the end of the last day of the shoot, we were exhausted. As we sat on the bus home, I noticed Erica was upset. I asked her why. With a disappointing voice she finally told me: "We haven't been paid yet." Someone told us our checks would come in the mail before too long. I did not know this at the time, but Erica already had plans for her money. She wanted one day to travel to St. Louis to meet James in person, but she was waiting for the right time to tell mother. She also wanted me to go with her. I remember her running to the mailbox twice a day hoping for a letter from James. (At that time our mail came twice a day.)

I had almost forgotten about my check by the time it actually arrived. Mother intercepted the checks before we even knew they came. Erica, however, saw them sitting on father's desk, where they were waiting to be deposited. Erica, suspecting something mischievous was in the works, took the checks and gave me mine. I didn't know what to do with a check and said I'd probably just give it to mother for safekeeping. "You'll never see your money again," Erica insisted, and persuaded me to open a bank account with her. We did, and for years, our money, five hundred Marks in all, sat in the bank.

***

One day in the summer of 1955, right before I reached my twenties birthday, I was relaxing on our balcony overlooking the lake when mother came outside with a newspaper. She showed me the article for a reunion weekend being held in town for people who had been displaced from Silesia. These were annual affairs, but we had never been to one. Communities that had been ripped apart by circumstance were slowly being knitted back together at these events. These meetings were held in the larger cities; desperate, separated families often went from meeting to meeting hoping to find their lost loved ones. This one was being held on a Sunday in Braunschweig.

Father opted to stay at home and smoke his cigars. So Erica, mother and I set out by car to the reunion. The event was not unlike a street fair: the huge tents that were set up for each different town of origin housed the crowds milling about, and gave it a similar feel.

There was, however, a sense of urgency and concentration that pervaded the crowd as people hunted for the tents of their hometowns. You felt as if you were being examined by every person you saw because you were scrutinizing each face, looking for familiar features, imagining the face to be younger.

Every so often, we thought we saw someone we knew or a face that seemed somehow familiar. Unless the person registered recognition as they looked at you, or unless you were overwhelmingly certain they were someone you knew, most of the time your impressions were misidentifications fueled by a desire to reconnect. We saw nobody we knew.

We searched under the tents for a table marked "Hummelstadt," hoping at least to leave our address there for someone in case we missed them, but we did not see one. After a few frustrating hours, we walked out to the edge of the crowd and sat outside at a nearby café for something to drink. Mother was about to give up on this year's reunion and suggested we head back to the car. Erica and I were tired and frustrated, too, but had not yet given up hope.

Suddenly, a voice called out from inside the café. "Frau Doctor! Frau Doctor!" A woman was approaching us. As she stepped outside into the sunlight I recognized her—-it was Hedwig! My eyes couldn't believe what I saw. All of a sudden, my thoughts from that terrible war had returned when I saw Hedwig again. She was the person who stood by us when mother was put in prison and raped. She was also the person who helped us through the darkest hours of our life during the war. She protected us when mother was not able to. She fed us, got us up, dressed us and was a surrogate mother. I also owe her that I am still alive today.

We leaped from our chairs to hug her. It was the purest moment of happiness I had experienced in the years since the war. Erica pulled up another chair and asked her to sit down. We sat down and took in the moment as she brought us up to date. More than ten years had passed since we had last seen Hedwig. Her hair was graying, and the young woman we had once known, had sprouted little wrinkles around the eyes and mouth. It was most certainly Hedwig, and I thought she looked beautiful.

After we had left, Hedwig stayed on at the mansion, where she worked six more months for the Goblinskys without pay. At one point, while she was shopping in town, she was arrested by Polish officers and taken to the police station for interrogation. She had remembered what had happened to mother and was rightly fearful for her life. She was put into a cell with other women who were taken out one at a time by men she did not recognize. She could hear them being beaten and probably raped. She had resigned herself to not struggle when one "interrogation" had ended with a gunshot.

Mother's lip trembled as Hedwig told the story; undoubtedly she was remembering what had happened to her. The thought of Hedwig experiencing those horrors terrified her. Hedwig had been detained for five hours or more before someone came for her. She did not recognize the man, but he recognized her from the Goblinsky's parties. Had Hedwig been a stranger, this man would have certainly raped or beaten her. Instead, the officer released her.

Hedwig did not return to the mansion after that. She left behind all of her belongings and fled straight to her mother's house. She thought Hummelstadt was no longer safe. She stayed with her mother for a couple of weeks, and then they were issued the same order to report to the train station that we received.

But the Polish people had asked her to stay behind, as she was such a good worker. It never crossed Hedwig's mind to leave her mother. She had tears in her eyes as she told us about the eviction; she remembered her poor kitty, Motte, looking at them through the window of the cottage as they walked away forever. She regretted not letting the cat go free. Perhaps someone would have taken her in.

Hedwig also told us our good girlfriend, Marianne Angelhorst, was left behind, and her mother had to leave without her. She got married to a Polish soldier. Also, younger people who were committed to work for the Polish order were allowed to stay. Many stories were told about how badly they were treated with hardly any pay and primitive housing. Again, sad memories of my childhood came pouring in as I remembered the old days. How could I ever forget them? Hedwig's parents were deported by cattle train like we were, but they were sent to Niedersachen. Eventually, they settled in Schweinfurt, where she currently lived.

After our reunion, Hedwig came by train often to visit us. She said many times she wanted to return to work for mother. We certainly would have been happy to have her back in our lives. Not long after we found Hedwig, Gisela gave her notice. When she left, Hedwig took her place, moving in and working full time and taking frequent trips to Schweinfurt to visit her mother.

Around this time, I started seeing a boy named Charlie. He was an English officer who was stationed in Hildesheim. We had met at the public swimming pool, where I had often admired him swimming the length of the pool alone. I didn't know he was English until I spoke to him. When we finally met, we hit it off immediately. He was tall and had dark brown hair and had beautiful, liquid brown eyes. He spoke German fairly well, and I spoke some English.

Our brief relationship was my first real interest and challenge in English, as we both found the task of communicating humorous and embarrassing. I think this commonality lowered our defenses somewhat, seeing someone in the same boat as we tried to make ourselves somewhat intelligible, or at least sound intelligible.

Erica liked him, but she hinted that she would be happy to pursue Wolfdieter, with whom I was still friends. If I had given up on him, she insinuated she would like to see him. ("I've never seen a more handsome boy," she said of him).

***

By now, Erica's ideas of leaving home became stronger every day. Erica had had enough, and she had made up her mind that she was determined to take her trip to America, no matter what mother said.

Throughout college, Erica had dragged me to see dozens of American movies (in English whenever possible) and had introduced me to American music. Eventually, I caught her enthusiasm for all things American, and even though I may have had a vague notion of how nice it might be to visit America one day, I never considered living there.

When Charlie told me he was going back home to London to be discharged from the Army, he invited me to visit him there. Erica saw a chance to persuade mother we wanted to do a little traveling. I was a little reluctant about traveling to the United States; it was so far away. Erica's intentions were to see if she could get some sort of work there. Her pen pal, in one of his long and touching letters (it was clear he had developed a crush on Erica during their correspondence), had offered to sponsor her if she came to the States. Erica was sure he would sponsor me, as well. I hesitated often and tried to talk myself out of it. In the end, my sister's persistence won. At least I would not be alone in a foreign country, and she would be a great comfort.

Mother really liked Charlie and probably heard wedding bells every time I had him over. After all, he was older than Wolfdieter, for one, and he had risen quickly through the ranks and commanded a large number of men in the British zone (where Hildesheim was). He also intended to follow his father into law when he returned to England. He did come and visit me twice in America later on, but I had lost interest in him, as I liked somebody else better during that time.

Mother thought Charlie might be a good match for me, and I used this strategy when I proposed the trip abroad. I told her Erica and I had been invited to London to stay with Charlie's family for a few weeks, and after that, Erica wanted to visit her pen pal in St. Louis. Mother thought that such a trip might not be such a bad thing, at least until Erica mentioned we would try to get jobs in St. Louis. After much discussion, she agreed to let us go to England, but the United States was simply not an option.

Erica, at this point, began a month-long badgering campaign to persuade mother to let us live abroad. Mother didn't have a moment's peace while Erica was around. You could hear Erica and mother's conversations throughout the house, almost invariably ending with my sister's promise, "We're going, no matter what."

One day, our parents summoned us to the main parlor to discuss our intentions and make an offer. "Why America?" she asked. She was clearly agonizing over the concession. "Why not Paris? You both speak French."

"We don't know anyone there," Erica replied.

"You don't know anyone in America."

"We know James."

"But that's just one person. I know several families in Paris. We can set you up to work there." That was exactly why we did not go to Paris, though mother did not know that. "Why do you have to go so far away? I mean, you're adults, but what makes you think America is somewhere you would like to live?"

I was surprised to hear mother refer to us as adults. I had never been accused of that before. My father was just sitting in his chair not saying a word. He was not the fighting type like my mother, as she was always the boss, anyway.

Erica had a list of reasons: to see the big cities, to improve her English (which was a compelling reason for mother), because of the financial opportunities (which was a compelling reason for father), to meet her friend in person, because it would be cheap to live there, and many other reasons.

Mother, infuriated and resigned to her daughters' betrayal, asked father for his opinion. Let them go, he nodded, but he was not looking so happy. "Once they see how hard it is working in another country, they'll be back." That clinched it for mother. She could not imagine us being successes in America, not without her. Mother said, "Well, you're making a big mistake," and left the room. She really didn't want us to leave, as she didn't want to lose us, after losing everything in the war.

***

The day of our departure for England finally arrived. The first leg of the trip, as far as Erica and I could tell, had no end. Erica was excited and impatient for our train to arrive at the station. I was excited too, but wondered whether or not I was making the right decision.

I had passively accepted that wherever Erica went, I would go, too. Most of that morning, however, was a blur.

My grandmother, Aunt Kaete and Hedwig had joined my parents at the station to see us off. They were all crying. My mother was crying and muttering, "You're making a big mistake." Even my father wiped a few tears that streamed down from behind his sunglasses. Wolfdieter, who said he would follow us to America, was not there. Hedwig snapped some pictures, but Erica was ecstatic. I tried to match her enthusiasm, but my heart pounded as I struggled to assure myself I was happy about leaving. I mean, I had made up my mind to go to America with Erica. Or had I?

When the train arrived, I suddenly felt an overpowering urge to beg to stay. But my family put us on the train, they kissed us good-bye, and let us go. We were free.

Epilogue: Hedwig's Visit to Hummelstadt in 1962

Hedwig told me much later, in 1962, that she took a bus tour to Silesia, to visit our mansion in Hummelstadt again. Hummelstadt is called Klodzski today, renamed by the Polish people. It was over seventeen years since Hedwig was there, when she was forced to work in our mansion for the Poles in 1945.

A secretary by the name of Baerbel, who worked in my father's office in Hummelstadt, arranged the whole trip. Although Hedwig left such terrible memories behind, she was strong and determined to go back. She was very interested to find out what had become of Hummelstadt and our mansion.

The whole trip included a bus ride, hotel, three meals a day, plus different sightseeing tours for six hundred DM. She got to stay in a hotel in Bad Altheide, for one whole week. Everyone had exchanged Marks for Polish money before, so they had some extra spending money. (The Polish money was in zlotys). She asked mother to go along, but she had no interest at all. She always said it would be too sad for her, and just couldn't be reminded of the devastating experiences during the war.

A huge bus filled with people from Hummelstadt was waiting for Hedwig at the train station in the early afternoon. She said there was only one empty seat left, so mother could not have joined her. The bus had to stop first in Helmstedt for visa checking, which took a very long time. The trip took all night, and finally early in the morning they arrived at the hotel in Bad Alteide, a resort town not too far from Hummelstadt.

Hedwig was surprised how our village had changed, but she still remembered many buildings in the town square, surrounded by trees which had become very large. She also noticed that many homes were in need of painting and repair. To her disbelief, Mittagessen was still served in the Schwesternhaus, the nun's house. This is the place where Erica and I went to kindergarten, when we were four years old. The Schwesternhaus had become a vacation place, which served food to visitors.

So Hedwig was served by the nuns for dinner only. She said the nuns all seemed very polite and proper. Hedwig was so happy to be back in Hummelstadt, she gave them a tip of 10.00 DM on the last day.

The food was okay too, but not particularly good. Many Polish people were trying very hard to copy the German dishes like goulash, wiener schnietzel, sauerbraten and others, but they never perfected it.

Hedwig also told me, that so many single, young Polish women wanted to become nuns, because they were well taken care of at the monastery. The waiting list, to be accepted, was very long.

Around this time, Poland was experiencing increasing economic and political difficulties. Everything was very expensive. Many people, who stayed behind, came over to the East zone for a few months in order to find some work as farmhands. They worked very hard, and were rewarded well with plenty of money, which meant that they could return home for a few months. They received DM for their farm work, which was more than Polish money at the time. Polish workers are known for their hard and efficient work.

Today, many German people live in Poland. Hedwig said the Polish people there don't want to be called Polish, but "Silesians."

Hedwig met a lady at the Schwesternhaus that she knew by the name of Hildegardt. She offered Hedwig a ride to see our mansion. Hedwig became very excited. When they entered the house, Hedwig noticed with wide-opened eyes, how much everything had changed. It seemed strange, yet very familiar to her.

At the front desk, a large, friendly lady with red curly hair, called Nathasha, greeted them in Polish. She was extremely polite, as she knew Frau Hildegardt. She spoke in broken German, but Hedwig was able to understand her well. She told Hedwig, that she would be happy to show her the apartments. For a moment, Hedwig's eyes lit up. She was confused, when the lady mentioned the word apartments.

The Polish people had made twelve two-bedroom apartments, out of our mansion. Each family had two rooms. The lady in the office politely asked Hedwig, if she would be interested in seeing them. She also informed Hedwig that she wouldn't be able to show her one of the apartments, as the gentleman who lived there was very strange. So Hedwig had the opportunity to visit eleven of the apartments, even on the very top floor, where three families lived. The apartments all looked so much alike.

A strong aroma came over them, as tenants were cooking Polish sausage. The two rooms were divided by a wall, and most of the families had beds, which could be put up during the day for sitting. I doubt if each family had a private bathroom. Hedwig did not ask.

Some apartments looked messy, with so much stuff all over the place. Others looked very neat and clean. Most people who opened the door were very polite. The red-headed manager of this mansion (our mansion), spoke Polish to them.

One apartment that Hedwig looked at had two small children. Hedwig gave them some chocolate that she brought along, hoping to give it to some children, who would think it was a treat. Curiously, Hedwig went out the back door, to see the rose garden. She couldn't believe what she saw. The grounds were covered with so many weeds that nobody would know it was once a beautiful rose garden. Some roses, however, were still peeking out between the tall brush. The familiar marble fountain, the centerpiece of the garden, was completely gone. Looking upward at the rear of the mansion, many people had their wash hanging out on the balconies to dry.

***

To immigrate to America was of course a very big decision to be made. Erica and I both were thrilled just thinking of doing something and making choices on our own, for the first time in our life. Simplicity was only a state of mind. The biggest force wasn't dealing with money. It was to explore our life on our own, not to be told by our mother what to, whom to date, where to go and what to wear. It wasn't really what we had and who we were, and what had made us happy. It was what we wanted to do about it. Of course, our enthusiasm, our drive, our ambition and curiosity had also a lot to do with it. We also wanted to meet people, who come from a different world. I guess, my story is also about hard choices and second chances. No doubt, that Erica was also the aggressive/persistent person and so stubborn. Was it because she was born one hour earlier than me? Already very early in life my father taught me the facts of life. He told us to work hard, be neat and clean and never give up on our dreams. Life is full of choices.

I felt very sad and I was heartbroken, when I boarded the train in Hildesheim on my way to England, leaving my family behind. I kept looking out the window as long as I could see my parents, who slowly disappeared from view, wiping my tears and almost crying. Erica and I were invited to   visit Charlie's parents in their beautiful home in London for two weeks, before we had planned our trip to America. We had traveled just about all over Europe with our parents, but we had never visited London before. I was very impressed with the city. My mother liked Charlie very much, and I was very fond of him, but many other things had crossed my mind at that time.

We had the chance to see life on our own. Erica decided that it was time to buy a car for both of us after we had been living in St. Louis for a while. As usual, it was her decision. Unfortunately, there was a slight problem: we didn't know how to drive a car, and we didn't have a driver's license. In Germany we were driven or picked up. We had paid $350.00 for that car. It was a very old Ford, gray in color, and not anything like my father's Mercedes we were used to. The ceiling on the back was slightly coming down and the seat cushions were in bad shape. Otherwise it drove just fine. We both were very proud of this car, because it belonged to us. I was happy when Erica got her driver's license first, but I was less happy when I found out that she not only flunked the driving test, but also had a car accident at the same time while the examiner was sitting next to her. Fortunately, she was not hurt.

Our parents were sending us plenty of money to live on and we weren't broke yet. But we definitely were thinking of getting jobs. My mother thought that we would return back home as soon as we were broke. Still, until she had died, she told me that she had never forgiven us for leaving Germany.

I had often wondered how far we had come to achieve independence. From the privileged life-style of the mansion, to the terrible times, the struggle and triumph we went through during the war, to the simple life in America. Life goes on. You can never bury the past, but you can create a new exciting life and not worry at the same time. For us each day was a new beginning, hoping for a fresh new start, an opportunity to fill bright hopes, and to achieve something.

In February of 1958 we boarded the ship America, for our journey to New York. Our first incident had already occurred when we nearly missed the train on our way to Southhampton, and from there our journey started. We had never been on a ship before. The weather was extremely stormy and cold. Erica got very sea-sick on the first day. I felt fine, but most people must have gotten sick in the dining room, for breakfast in the morning was left nearly empty. Erica was very relieved by touching ground again after a long ten days of suffering. I was amazed to see the Statue of Liberty, before we arrived at the port. I was most impressed with so many tall buildings on the skyline.

Our sponsor, Jim, was waiting for us at the port in New York. From there we headed straight by car to St. Louis. Erica had noticed that Jim had fallen in love with her, which made her feel very uncomfortable. She liked him very much but only as a friend. We had spent about a week in a hotel in St. Louis, before we were able to find a place to live. Jim wanted to take us to Hannibal, Missouri, which is only about three hours distance from St. Louis, to stay with his parents. They owned a bakery and he thought that maybe we would like to work there one day and also he could get closer to Erica, but she wasn't interested. In St. Louis we lived in small, one bedroom apartments on Waterman Street. Unfortunately, we kept moving from one place to another, as most places were unbelievably dirty and filthy, occupied with mice. We were kept so busy with scrubbing and cleaning those dirty places, that our friends would make fun of us, telling us that we had nearly cleaned the whole Waterman Street. Eventually we found a little nicer place, and Erica recommended that we take in a roommate. But to our disappointment our roommate didn't work out either. We discovered that this young lady was a prostitute, and entertained men during the day, while we were working. She eventually moved out, and stole almost all my nice nightgowns.

Jim, our sponsor, took us downtown in St. Louis to have an interview at the International Shoe Company to find a job for us. We girls had never worked before in our entire lives. The interview went well. The boss, a nice looking, middle-aged man with dark glasses, asked us what we wanted to do. After finding out about our education, he smiled and told us that he would train us on the big IBM machines as keypunch operators, as data entry processors. It didn't take us long to learn all about it, and our boss was very pleased with our work. The nice boss called us back to his office and awarded us with frequent raises. I also liked the people we were working with. Some would invite us to their homes for dinner. We would also have Jim over for dinner casually. We kept writing to our parents regularly, as we had promised. We had learned to show respect and be considerate towards our parents. Good manners and courtesy had not faded in our generation. I had really not too much time to get homesick, as we kept so busy. But we were very happy when each Christmas a big parcel from our parents filled with German schokolade (chocolate) was waiting for us at the front door. That was the only time I wished I could have celebrated Christmas with my family at home.

We were very happy with our jobs and we had been working there for nearly a year. Erica kept looking in the newspapers for a more exciting and adventurous job. We heard that Ozark Airlines in St. Louis was hiring flight attendants. We had to somehow figure out how to get the time off for an interview, as we had to work during the day. It was Erica's idea to tell our boss that we both had a dentist appointment that day. Our boss was smiling and he knew what we were up to, dressed up in our best Easter outfits. We were so nervous and excited when we received the phone call, that we were hired;

Erica dropped the telephone receiver on the floor! We became the first Ozark employees.

From that day on our lives changed. We both loved flying and the very nice people around us. Ozark Airlines was a small, but a wonderful airline to work for, it later became TWA and than American Airlines. We moved to a small house close to the airport and bought a dog. He was a German shepherd named Prince. Life was getting better for us. We made many friends and frequented a club called "International Institute" which only foreigners were able to attend. Our friends often took us to the Playboy Club. Once we were sitting at the same table with Hugh Heffner, founder of the Playboy Club.

During our flying time, we had the chance to visit Germany more often, but we would never go home together, as we didn't want Prince left alone at home. But it happened only once, when we both were selected by the airline industry to attend the International Airline convention (ALTA) for one week in Amsterdam.

We both got married to American men while we were flying and living pretty close to each other, and a day didn't pass by without seeing each other. I was very happy that Erica had decided to let me keep Prince, although we both loved this dog very much. But soon after that, Erica suddenly showed up with the biggest dog I had ever seen in my life. He was nearly as big as a pony. It was an Irish wolfhound, a very friendly dog with beautiful large eyes and his tail would never stop wagging!

One day I noticed that Erica was not feeling well and she had lost some weight. I was very concerned and I worried about her a lot. One morning when she showed up on a flight, she told me how bad she really felt. This went on for quite some time and she would never miss a flight with me. She worked as hard as ever and nobody had really noticed how sick she really was. When she was finally admitted to a hospital, she was diagnosed with ovarian cancer and the doctors gave her three months to live. She died on Christmas day in 1971. That was the biggest shock for me, as we both were so close and had gone through so much together. It was very hard on me and just about impossible to accept. I quit the airline job one year later, after flying for ten years, after I was pregnant with my daughter Tanja. At that time we were not able to fly if we were pregnant.

I do not regret leaving home, and I have no intention of ever returning to Europe. There are times when I miss Germany: the culture, the classical music and the beautiful flowers. I miss visiting the big cities that have so many outdoor cafes. In 1989, right after the Wall came down, I visited Berlin again. I had visited West Germany many times since I moved to the States. It was almost unimaginable to me, that I could pass through the Brandenburg Gate freely. I could see the difference between East and West Berlin. The Western half of the city was built up, a modern city, but the East was run-down and tired. You could see scars left by the artillery on the facades of the buildings. Soon, a forest of scaffolding would spring up in the East, as the long divided nation pursued true reunification. But Hummelstadt would never be part of Germany again, like much of Silesia, it is now Polish. At any rate, I am not sure that I could recognize the town of my birth.

***

As I look back on my childhood, I have often, wondered what my childhood would have been like without the war. Would I have left Germany, and remained in Hildesheim with my family? Often my memories come back like a foggy dream. I can't help thinking about all those years, even though it was such a long time ago. World War II will never be forgotten, and it has left a wound which can never be healed.

It often seems strange how a little girl from Hummelstadt remembers the devastating experiences of that destructive war.

I grew up very fast. Being much older now, I think of many things-people, politics, government, social dignity, much differently, now. I remember my mother's principles and coaching, when we were young, and why she was so determined. I have learned so much from those terrible experiences, and now can share with my children some of the good memories. I have learned that one day you have everything, and the next day all possessions, your life, your dignity, your soul, can be stolen. You can live a wonderful life, and suddenly you have lost everything. Your routine, your schedule, all the familiar things, can be taken away very easily, but the memories remain. Too many people fail to appreciate what they have, and they take it for granted, until, one day, they might have lost it all.

The war affected different people in a different way. Sometimes, I still dream about different events, and memories, and heartaches, and I still find it difficult to talk about my terrible experiences of the war, without having tears in my eyes.

My children would often ask me questions about the war, and the terrible events I experienced. I would always tell them the simple plain truth, "Yes, it was worse than anybody could ever imagine. It was even worse than that."